women's MINISTRY
in the 21st century

Loveland, Colorado

Group resources actually work!

This Group resource helps you focus on **"The 1 Thing™"**— a life-changing relationship with Jesus Christ. "The 1 Thing" incorporates our **R.E.A.L.** approach to ministry. It reinforces a growing friendship with Jesus, encourages long-term learning, and results in life transformation, because it's:

Relational
Learner-to-learner interaction enhances learning and builds Christian friendships.

Experiential
What learners experience through discussion and action sticks with them up to 9 times longer than what they simply hear or read.

Applicable
The aim of Christian education is to equip learners to be both hearers and doers of God's Word.

Learner-based
Learners understand and retain more when the learning process takes into consideration how they learn best.

Women's Ministry in the 21st Century
The Encyclopedia of Practical Ideas
Copyright © 2004 Group Publishing, Inc.

Visit our Web site: **www.grouppublishing.com**

Credits
Editor: Beth Robinson
Creative Development Editor: Dave Thornton
Chief Creative Officer: Joani Schultz
Copy Editor: Alison Imbriaco
Art Director: Pamela Poll
Print Production Artist: Pamela Poll
Cover Art Director/Designer: Jeff A. Storm
Illustrator: Jane Mjolsness
Production Manager: Peggy Naylor

Unless otherwise noted, Scripture taken from the HOLY BIBLE, NEW INTERNATIONAL VERSION®. Copyright © 1973, 1978, 1984 by International Bible Society. Used by permission of Zondervan Publishing House. All rights reserved.

Library of Congress Cataloging-in-Publication Data
Women's ministry in the 21st century : the encyclopedia of practical ideas.-- 1st American pbk. ed.
     p. cm.
 ISBN 0-7644-2700-8 (pbk. : alk. paper)
 1. Women in church work. 2. Women--Religious aspects--Christianity. I. Title: Women's ministry in the twenty-first century. II. Group Publishing.

 BV4415.W648 2004
 259'.082--dc22

                        2004007723

10 9 8 7 6 5 4 3 2 1   13 12 11 10 09 08 07 06 05 04
Printed in the United States of America.

contents

section **two: serving others** **37**

section **three: spiritual growth** **61**

section **nine: leader helps** 213

contributors

Many thanks to the following women who serve the women in their churches faithfully and who contributed dozens of wonderful women's ministry ideas to this book.

Linda Olson, of Desert Vineyard Christian Fellowship in Lancaster, California

Holly Stevenson, Jane Carter, Diane Roberts, Idella Meyers, and Rocio Bates, of East Hill Church in Gresham, Oregon

Pat Rohach, of Southland Christian Church in Lexington, Kentucky

Christy Harrell, of Peoples Church in Salem, Oregon

Christy Morr and **Rebecca Smith**, of First Evangelical Free Church in Fullerton, California

Doris Lee Aldag, of Upper Arlington Lutheran Church in Columbus, Ohio

Pamela Gilsenan, of Vineyard Church in Fort Collins, Colorado

introduction

Welcome to *Women's Ministry in the Twenty-First Century: The Encyclopedia of Practical Ideas*!

We believe that God passionately loves women and has a wonderful purpose in mind for them. Women are strong, resourceful, passionate, and loving. When women give themselves completely to God's service, watch out, 'cause amazing things are going to happen!

The ideas in this book will help you guide the women in your church to love God with their whole heart; to love their sisters in Christ with a pure, strong love; and to zealously serve the church and the world around them with a sweet, self-sacrificing spirit.

Within these pages, you'll find dozens and dozens of fantastic ideas that you can use with the women in your church today. These ideas are practical, hands-on, and experiential. Whether you need a devotion for your holiday banquet or a service project for your young mom's group, this book has it.

We pray that the women in your church will reap eternal benefits from the ideas in this book. May God bless you and your ministry in his name.

fellowship AND FUN

Women love to have fun! It almost goes without saying that all of the activities you plan for women need to be enjoyable. But fellowship and fun have a deeper purpose.

In today's culture, women long for a connection with others. Women are often desperately lonely. People move more frequently than they did a generation ago, and it takes a long time to rebuild satisfying friendships after a move. Women who stay at home often feel isolated. Their families may live far away, and neighbors don't get to know one another they way they once did.

Those who work outside the home may have acquaintances at work, but these relationships are not often deep, abiding friendships. Since these women frequently spend their evenings catching up on household chores, they don't have much time to build friendships.

However, the church is to be built on relationships and community. The Bible says more than once that we are the body of Christ—

we are all connected. We are family. In fact, the Bible goes so far as to say that we belong to one another. Unfortunately, this kind of close bond is not very many people's experience at church. Consider your own church. How many people come to your church, attend the worship service, and then leave the church building without ever speaking to anyone, other than to say "good morning" to the greeter at the door? People can (and do!) attend a church for decades without ever being invited into true community. This should not be!

Think what our churches would be if people were truly loved and cared for from the moment they entered the door. How would our churches be different if people welcomed one another into their lives and their homes? How would the community react if Christians really were known by their love for one another?

One of your jobs as a women's ministry director is to help women build deep, lasting ties with other women in the church and discover a sense of belonging in the church. Women must learn to support one another and to draw support from other Christian women. They must learn to bear one another's burdens and to love one another with Christ's love. And women must also learn to be joyful and carefree. It's your job to help every woman in your church discover how we are mysteriously and wonderfully interconnected and interdependent. Providing a foundation for these lessons means developing opportunities for women to be with one another for no other purpose than to laugh, to learn about one another, and to make friends.

In our modern culture, people can feel very alone. Not only do people move far from their families, they've forgotten how to make friends. They often need to be guided through the process of learning, sharing, talking, and becoming vulnerable to another. That's why these activities are so important. They give women opportunities for connections that they may not know how to create on their own.

Of course, your program can't end here. It needs to provide balance. If all your programs are just for fun, women will miss out on the chance to grow in knowledge and faith. On the other hand, if all your programs emphasize learning, the women in your church will be lacking in love. Love is the primary Christian virtue; it's to be our primary activity.

Read these activities through carefully. Let all this information percolate in your mind over several days and be open to the leading of the Spirit. Use these activities as they are, or let them spark your imagination. Most important, though, have fun, love one another, and draw other women to Christ and the church through sincere love and fellowship.

IDEA 1
welcoming ideas

Do whatever it takes to ensure that women are welcomed into your group and that they have the opportunity to form deep, lasting friendships. Here are some ideas.

• **Form a welcoming committee.** Find friendly people to greet women at the door, to explain what the agenda is for the day, and to chat with people before the day's event gets started.

• **Introduce the leaders.** Make sure that each woman who addresses the group introduces herself and tells the whole group about her role in the women's ministry. Don't assume that everyone knows who the leaders are.

• **Provide clear, complete information about your women's ministry programs.** It's easy to come up with catchy titles for programs and neglect to explain what those programs are for, when they meet, where they meet, and how long meetings last. Don't assume that everyone knows, for example, that all regular Bible studies take a break during the month of December—be very clear about the details.

• **Form a friend-making team.** Do more than just greet women at the door. Form a team of friendly women to purposefully look for women they don't know and engage them in warm, friendly conversation. It won't matter if women on the friend-making team end up talking to women who have been coming to your church for months or years. The friend-making team will serve two purposes: It will help to get women connected in real friendships, and it will encourage women to move outside their regular group of friends. For the women on this friend-making team, connecting with women they don't know should take precedence over chatting with their old friends.

• **Don't expect too much right away.** It can be easy to ask new people to bare their souls and sign away their lives to the women's ministry, but that can scare people away, especially those who are new to church. Be friendly, warm, and accepting. Offer sincere friendship. Offer as much information as you can about your programs. But also respect people's privacy by allowing them to ease into programs as they feel comfortable.

• **Provide many entry points for service.** The women who will feel most connected to others will always be the women who volunteer to help plan and serve. Allow plenty of opportunities for women new to the church to get involved.

• **Watch out for cliques.** This isn't just a problem with junior high girls. It's just natural for women to form closer friendships with some women than with others. But watch your programs and your events closely. If you notice that the same women always sit together and that other women always sit alone, come up with a plan to shake up the seating and help women interact with new people.

• **Don't just watch the numbers.** It's easy to assume that well-attended programs are successful. But it may be that women come to event after event without ever truly connecting with another human being. Provide discussion time at every event, and encourage women to chat in pairs or trios to help them get to know one another. Also be sure to have a balance of large group opportunities and small group opportunities. Always try to help women deepen their connections to the group by getting involved with a smaller group of women that meets regularly.

IDEA 2
weeknight brown-bag meal

Invite the single women in your church to a once-a-week brown-bag meal. Each woman should pack her own dinner (or bring take out) and come to the church or someone's home for a time of fellowship and discussion. Be sure to plan for child care so that single moms can attend.

Plan a topic of discussion for each meeting. For example, you might plan to discuss "What do I look for in a romantic partner?" or "How do I incorporate prayer into my everyday life?" Allow time for women to eat and enjoy the company instead of the usual eating alone at home. Then introduce the topic of conversation. You may also want to plan a short devotion or a time of worship.

These meetings will provide an ideal setting for making new friends. The brown-bag meals will also help single women form networks that can help them find roommates or jobs, share rides, and find Christian support and accountability. And brown-bag meals provide a great opportunity for women to invite other single women (neighbors, co-workers, sisters) to a nonthreatening church activity.

You might also use this idea for other groups of women, such as single moms or widows.

IDEA 3
bike clinic

Encourage the women in your church to come to a bike clinic. Invite local bike mechanics (women, if possible) to give simple maintenance tips, including how to do a tuneup and how to fix a flat tire. Arrange for the mechanics to help women "size" their bikes and adjust handlebars and seats for a better fit and a more comfortable ride.

Provide table displays with information about biking gear and clothing, local bike paths, and biking-to-work opportunities.

Before the event, encourage women to donate used bikes to be given away to other women at the event. Give the bikes away by drawing names out of a hat. Women can also use this event to pass along no-longer-needed baby seats and helmets to other women. Be sure that the bike mechanics inspect the seats and the helmets for safety. A helmet that's sustained an impact in a crash should not be handed on.

While women use this time to get to know other women in the church who enjoy cycling, take advantage of the opportunity to plan several rides in your area along established, paved trails or, for the more adventurous, on unpaved trails. Encourage the cyclists to meet at least once a month to enjoy fellowship and ride together.

IDEA 4
birthday limousine

Treat the women in your women's ministry like VIPs. It's a great way to reward women who've been faithful servants in your women's ministry program or just to encourage women with a little bit of extra pampering.

Once a month, have a limousine pick up the women who celebrate birthdays during that month and deliver them to your regular women's ministry meeting in style. Call all of the women a week in advance to confirm their intention to attend the event. Then, on the day of the event, have the limousine pick up each woman either at her home or place of business.

On occasion, friends of the birthday woman might enjoy "dressing to the nines" and renting the limo for additional time so they can take her out for a fabulous meal—at a favorite fast-food restaurant.

One side benefit of this VIP treatment is the "advertising" your women's ministry program will get. Neighbors and co-workers are sure to ask the birthday women about the limousine, and their questions would lead naturally to a conversation about how much fun your church's women's ministry is.

IDEA 5
overnight getaways

Plan times for small groups of women (four to ten) to go on short getaways. If you live near a popular vacation destination, an overnight trip can be very affordable if four women can share a room and get away on short notice. In the winter, plan to snowshoe, sled, or skate during the day and spend the evenings in the Word and the hot tub. In the summer, hike, swim, or laze on the beach. Trips can be planned for one or two nights, depending on family and work schedules. Make the trips easy on the budget by planning simple meals that can be heated in a microwave or by eating in the hotel's dining room. You may want to prepare Bible study lessons ahead of time, or you may want to simply let each woman have uninterrupted time for her own prayer and study.

IDEA 6
widows craft group

Begin a weekly craft group for older widows in your congregation. This group could prevent these women from being isolated and provide the support and friendship they need. For suitable craft ideas, look in magazines, in fabric or hobby stores, or on the Web.

The women might come together at the church or at someone's home to work on their crafts. They may want to chat while they work, or they may choose to listen to a teaching tape or to Christian music while they work. Another idea is listening to one woman as she reads the Bible or another Christian book during the work time.

The women might make crafts for themselves, or they might choose to make crafts to use to cheer up people in a nursing home or retirement facility. For example, one group created place cards and table decorations for holiday celebrations and other monthly celebrations at a local nursing home.

IDEA 7
praise and exercise

Encourage women to get together once a week at the church building for praise and exercise. Gather a variety of praise and exercise CDs, videos, and DVDs. Turn up the music, and enjoy exercising together.

Choose a rotating team of facilitators, and suggest that whoever facilitates chooses the exercise video that week. Encourage women to drop in whenever they can. You may want to plan the meeting early in the morning so that women with jobs can join and still get to work on time. Work-at-home women can linger for a fruit and coffee breakfast. Or plan the exercise time for late morning or for a lunch hour.

IDEA 8
prayer walks

Find a peaceful walking path in your town; many towns have walking paths along rivers. Invite small groups of women to gather to walk and pray together. You'll want to schedule at least two weekly walking times. For example, you might want to provide an early morning time and a lunch hour time. Encourage the groups to stay small. It's best if women walk and pray in groups of no more than three or four. Encourage the women to pray for one another, for the church, and for the prayer requests of individuals in your women's ministry.

IDEA 9
community progressive dinner

Once a year, plan a progressive dinner with the other women's ministries in your community. The dinner is easy to plan, and it will draw the women of Christ together in greater unity.

You'll need the participation of at least two other churches, and you'll need to start planning a couple of months in advance. The number of churches will determine how many courses you serve. Possible courses are appetizers, soup, salad, main course, and dessert. Each church should serve its course at its church building. During your planning meeting, pick a date, choose a menu, decide which church will serve which course, and plan a short devotional to be given during the dessert course (see pages 73-79 for ideas). You'll also want to plan for some fun getting-to-know-you questions (see page 23 for ideas) for the women to discuss during each course.

Start advertising your event and take reservations. Each church can absorb the cost of its course, so you need not charge a fee, though you may want to make arrangements for the other churches to chip in a bit for the church that provides the main course, as that tends to be more expensive.

Be sure to use disposable plates, cups, and flatware for this event to minimize cleanup. Encourage each church to decorate its tables creatively. At the first course, arrange the seating so that the women will be sitting next to women from other churches. Ask God's blessing for the evening and thank him for the food. Have the women discuss one of the getting-to-know-you questions while they eat.

Then have everyone continue on to the next church for the next course. Have the women sit with different people from the other churches for the second course, and have them discuss another one of the getting-to-know-you questions while they eat. Continue doing this at each church. End the evening with a short devotion and a closing prayer. Encourage the women to continue getting to know the women they met at this event.

IDEA 10
ice-cream sundae

Devote one women's ministry event completely to ice cream. Serve a gigantic ice-cream sundae feast! Set out buckets of ice cream on long tables, and then set out all of the ingredients you can think of to use as toppings. Encourage women to eat as much ice cream as their stomachs will hold.

Set up small tables around the room, and appoint a table captain at each table to help the women get to know one another. It's a good idea to encourage women to sit and chat with someone they don't already know.

This is an easy event for women to bring friends to.

If you'd like, include a short program including a devotion and a time of prayer. (See pages 73-83 for ideas.)

IDEA 11
getting-to-know-you questions

• As a child, what did you want to be when you grew up?
• What was your mom's best meal when you were a kid?
• What would people be surprised to find out about you?
• How would you describe the perfect life?
• Did you plan your wedding when you were a child? What was it like?
• What was your favorite music group when you were a teenager? Do you still listen to the group?
• What's the perfect vacation? Have you ever had the perfect vacation?
• What do you think God looks like?
• Would you rather read books or magazines? What's your favorite thing to read?
• What was your biggest flop in the kitchen?
• How many pairs of shoes do you own? Is that number enough?
• How many times in your life have you moved?
• What part of the newspaper do you read first? Why?
• Which meal do you like best: breakfast, lunch, or dinner?
• How many siblings do you have? Where are they now?
• What brought you to this church? How long have you been here?
• What is your favorite outfit? Why?
• Have you kept up with your high school or college friends? Why or why not?
• What's your favorite way to spend a weekend?
• Are your photos neatly organized or all in a pile?

IDEA 12
jammin'

Form praise groups of women who like to sing or play instruments. The groups can get together just for fun—to play music together and worship God. Or the groups can play music for the women's ministry events at your church. The groups can also provide music at local nursing homes, retirement centers, preschools, or hospitals.

IDEA 13
bath sundaes

Make these cute "bath sundaes" to sell as a fundraiser or to give as gifts to the women in your group. The craft idea is also a great project to add to a regular meeting.

For each woman you'll need:
- ice-cream parfait glass
- 2/3 cup bath salts
- reclosable plastic bag
- nylon-net bath pouf
- bath-oil ball
- cellophane or clear plastic gift wrap
- ribbon

Place the bath salts in the plastic bag, squish out the air, and close the bag. Put the bag in the bottom of the parfait glass. Place the bath pouf on top so the string is on the underside. Place the bath-oil ball on top of the bath pouf (to represent the cherry). Place the glass on a sheet of cellophane. Bring the cellophane up around the bath sundae, and wrap the sundae tightly enough that the pouf and the bath-oil ball don't fall off. Tie with a pretty ribbon.

IDEA 14
apple-pie class

Offer a class on basic pie making to the women in your group. Ask an older woman who is known for her scrumptious baking to teach the class. Hold the class either at her home or in the church kitchen. You'll probably want to keep the class to about five women. Gather enough rolling pins, pie pans, mixing bowls, and pie ingredients for all the women. Have the teacher guide her students through making the pies. While the pies are cooking and after the kitchen is clean, have the women chat and get to know one another better. Then have the women enjoy the teacher's pie and take their own pies home to their families.

You can offer similar classes on bread making, knitting, quilting, gardening, and sewing.

IDEA 15
flower-bed fun

Perhaps the landscape surrounding your church could be brightened up with flower beds. Get permission from the groundskeeper at your church to add flower beds or to take over the maintenance of the beds already there.

If you'll be adding flower beds, work with a group of experienced gardeners to plan what to plant. Run your plan by the church board to make sure your plans are OK.

Then have small groups of women take responsibility for the planting, care, and maintenance of the flower beds, one or two flower beds per small group, throughout the growing season.

The gardening groups can provide opportunities for women to learn about gardening from the seasoned gardeners in your women's ministry.

IDEA 16
network of women

The women in your group have a wealth of skills and talents. Share the wealth by putting together a booklet listing all the women in your church and the skills they're willing to share with others. Make it clear, however, that there should be no charge for these services; the booklet is not a business directory. The idea is for women to come alongside one another and to help other women learn how to do these skills.

The women in your group might be willing to help with such things as:
- mending and sewing
- baking
- weeding
- budgeting
- car maintenance
- pottery
- decorating
- fitness and nutrition

- investing
- landscaping
- flower arranging

IDEA 17
post-a-note board

Encourage the women in your church to share their lives and their needs with one another with this great bulletin-board idea.

Place a large bulletin board in the area where your women generally meet. You may need to have a bulletin board that can be stored between meetings.

Divide the bulletin board into different sections with headings such as "Prayer Requests," "For Sale," "Wanted," and "Free for the Taking." Place 3x5 cards and pens nearby, and encourage women to post a note when they have a need in their life or a service to offer. For example, someone might post a note when her garden has produced too much zucchini or someone might post a note if she needs help finding a used prom dress for her daughter.

Be sure to review the board frequently to make sure no inappropriate notes have been posted.

IDEA 18
book clubs

Encourage fellowship among the book lovers in your group by helping them form book clubs.

Groups should choose and read a new book every month and then get together to discuss the book. If the women in the group decide to share the hosting responsibilities, they should determine who will host the next meeting before the end of each meeting. The host gets to pick the book to be read.

Here are some great books to get groups started:

Gift From the Sea by Anne Morrow Lindbergh
Girl With the Pearl Earring by Tracy Chevalier
The Great Divorce by C.S. Lewis
How Green Was My Valley by Richard Llewellyn
The Poisonwood Bible by Barbara Kingsolver
Traveling Mercies by Anne Lamott (This book includes strong

language, but it's a moving collection of essays and stories about a woman's journey toward faith in Christ.)

Strong Poison by Dorothy L. Sayers

The Red Tent by Anita Diamant

Fahrenheit 451 by Ray Bradbury

A Christmas Carol by Charles Dickens

The Remains of the Day by Kazuo Ishiguro

IDEA 19
weight-loss group

Lots of women would like help with losing a few pounds, and all women can benefit from making new friends. Encourage the women to get together once a month to share tips and recipes and to give one another support and encouragement.

The women may want to put a dollar into a pot at each meeting and then weigh in. Have the women bring in the same scale each week, and have someone keep a log of each woman's weight loss to help the weighing in be as accurate as possible. The woman who has lost the most weight gets to choose a ministry to donate the money to.

IDEA 20
where do you live?

Display a large map of your community on a bulletin board near the area where your women's ministry meets. Place pins, flags, and pens nearby. Encourage the women to jot their names on little flags and pin the flags on the map to show where they live.

Leave the map out at every women's ministry meeting so the women can study the map to see who lives close to them. Encourage women to make friends with women who live near them.

Adapt this activity by displaying a map women can use to show where their kids go to school.

IDEA 21
interviews

Make interviews a regular part of your women's ministry gatherings to help women get to know one another better.

Choose a different woman to spotlight each time. Let her know at least a couple of weeks in advance that you'd like to interview her in front of the group.

During the interview, introduce the woman to the group. Then ask her questions. For example, you might ask,

- How long have you lived here?
- What brought you to this church?
- Where did you grow up?
- Did you go to college? What did you study?
- What were your dreams as a young person?
- What do you do with your days?
- Tell us about your family.
- What are your hobbies and interests?
- What do you like best about the women's ministry programs here?

You can adapt this interview to the pastors and other staff members at your church to help the women get to know them better.

IDEA 22
thanksgiving pies

Make and sell homemade pies for Thanksgiving. Take orders (no more than five pies per person) two to three weeks before the holiday. Then spend the three days before the holiday baking the pies together at the church. You can either deliver the pies or have people pick them up at the church.

Consider charging six dollars for pecan pie and five dollars for pumpkin, apple, and berry pies. If women in the group donate the supplies, your profits will be higher.

While your women's ministry makes money, women in the group will have a great time getting to know one another and deepening friendships as they work together.

IDEA 23
scrapbooking club

Many women are passionate about scrapbooking. Form small groups of scrapbookers who can meet weekly or monthly in one another's homes. Then, several times a year, offer "scrap fever" events at the church, and invite all the scrapbookers to gather for a full day of scrapbooking. Set up tables so women can work four people per table. Make sure each table has a supply of brochures that describe all of the women's ministry events and programs, as well as all of your church's ministries.

Have women bring their own supplies and snacks. Encourage women to bring their non-Christian friends who are passionate about scrapbooking. You can give away scrapbooking tools and supplies as door prizes, and have local experts give demonstrations on new techniques. At the end of the event, encourage the women to display their scrapbooks, and allow fifteen minutes to half an hour for all the women to wander through the room and look at all the scrapbooks.

If the women in your church enjoy scrapbooking, consider using these resources from Group's Scripture Scrapbooks™ line to form a regular scrapbooking Bible study group: *Christian Living From A to Z, Fruit of the Spirit,* and *God's Good Gifts.*

IDEA 24
basket exchange

Almost every woman has a collection of baskets at home. As a special gift exchange, suggest that women find a basket at home, purchase a gift that would be suitable for any woman, and put the gift in the basket. Put a spending limit of five dollars on the gifts. One woman's gift might be homemade pancake mix, syrup, and a new spatula. Another woman might put potting soil and flower seeds in her basket.

When the women arrive at the event, put a numbered sticky dot on each basket. Place all the baskets at the front of the room on tables. Pass a hat so that women can draw a number from the hat, go to the table, and find the basket with that number. If a woman gets her own basket, have her draw another number.

IDEA 25
manicure party

This idea works best with groups of ten or fewer. And it works better if you hold this event in someone's home.

Have everyone bring in their nail-care and hand-care products.

For example, at least one woman could bring in her paraffin hand spa. Others can bring in lotions and exfoliating creams; for example, Mary Kay offers a four-step hand-care system. Others can bring their collections of nail polish.

Then have fun doing each other's nails. Women can experiment with colors that are bolder than colors they'd normally try. You can also experiment with stencils and stickers. Women can try as many shades as they want—it's easy to just take off one color and put on another.

This is a just-for-fun event that gives women a chance to get together, chat, and relax. You might want to watch a fun movie while everyone's nails are drying.

IDEA 26
monster salad party

This is a great party for a summertime just-for-fun get-together, and it's great for a large group of women.

You'll need a brand-new, small, plastic swimming pool and lots of aluminum foil. Completely cover the swimming pool with the foil.

Invite women to come to a salad party. Have each woman bring one bag of salad greens and one or two pounds of other salad vegetables cut in small pieces. Some women might provide extras such as bacon bits, chopped hard-boiled eggs, and shredded cheese. Have the church provide several salad dressings, crackers, fresh bread, and beverages, as well as plates and tableware.

Put the foil-covered swimming pool on a large table. As the women arrive, have them put their greens and veggies into the swimming pool. Toss the salad well before eating. Put the bacon bits, eggs, and cheese in small bowls next to the swimming pool. Set out the dressings, crackers, and bread. Have beverages available at all the tables.

IDEA 27
picture gallery

Periodically through the year, invite one or two women to provide a "picture gallery" of their lives. Give each of the chosen women two or three sheets of poster board. Have the women choose snapshots from their lives to mount on the poster board. The women can choose pictures from childhood all the way up to the present. Have the women include pictures of their vacations, their families, their hobbies, and anything else that would help the other women know more about their lives. Have the women write captions under each snapshot to explain what's happening in each photo.

Display each woman's picture gallery on an easel or on the wall at various women's ministry events. As women arrive at events, invite them to look at the picture galleries to get to know the spotlighted women better.

The picture galleries provide a great way to make use of the time between the first arrivals and the beginning of the event. Keep track of the women you've spotlighted, and strive to include all the regulars in your women's ministry over the course of several years.

IDEA 28
meals to go

Form a team of women who can provide meals to other women when they need help. For example, the team can provide meals when women are sick, when they have babies, or when they or their husbands have lost jobs.

To make this even more fun, though, have the women agree to give away home-cooked meals at your women's ministry events. Have women who come to an event put their names in a box. Choose one name from the box. During the next week, the meals team should provide the winner with a wonderful home-cooked meal, including a main course, a salad, bread, and a dessert. It's also nice to include pretty paper goods so the recipient doesn't have to do dishes that night. Add all the little touches that will make the meal special.

Encourage the team to always provide home-cooked meals when they provide meals. Cooking a meal is much nicer and friendlier than just picking up a bucket of chicken from the drive-through.

Whoever delivers the meal should take a few minutes to visit with the recipient of the meal. This is an easy way for women to extend friendship and love to one another.

You can also use this idea to welcome new women into your group. A home-cooked meal would be an especially nice way to welcome someone who's just moved to your area.

You might also adapt this idea and form a housecleaning team. Organize a group of women who enjoy housework and who would love to get to know one another as they serve others by cleaning the houses of women who could use a helping hand.

IDEA 29
welcome wagon

Moving to a new town can be very difficult. Put together a team of friendly women to welcome new families to your town or to your church's neighborhood.

First, find out who's new in your church's neighborhood or in your town by consulting a local real estate office for lists of newly sold homes. Many realtors compile these lists by neighborhood each month or each quarter.

Put together welcome baskets including information about the area, such as

- the location and hours of business of the local post office and library,
- the location of the best local restaurants,
- your city's best festivals and special events,
- your city's best parks,
- your city's best recreational facilities,
- good beauticians,
- your city's best doctors and dentists,
- where to get the best deals at local stores and markets, and
- your church's ministry information.

Include something home-baked, such as muffins or cookies.

Ask the friendliest women in your ministry to deliver the baskets and stay just long enough to introduce themselves and welcome the new family to the area. Encourage the women to check back with the family after a week or so, just to see if they have questions about the neighborhood or your church.

If you can, coordinate the "welcome wagon" so that women "welcomers" live within a block or two of the new family. This will promote friendships between neighbors and a spirit of community.

IDEA 30
early morning breakfast groups

Finding time to get together for fun can be difficult for women.

For some women, the easiest time to get together might be early in the morning when the rest of the family is still asleep. Form an early morning breakfast group for these women. Find an inexpensive breakfast spot, and encourage the women to meet there as early as 6 a.m. for a time of fellowship. Encourage the group to meet weekly.

Other women might find that the easiest time to meet is during the lunch hour.

IDEA 31
women's ministry directory

Help the women get to know one another with this women's ministry directory.

Photocopy the form on page 34, enlarging it by about 15 percent. Ask each woman in your women's ministry to fill out a form as completely as possible. Then gather all the forms, make copies, and put them in inexpensive, plastic three-ring binders.

Always have blank forms available at your women's ministry events so that new women can fill out a form and be included in the directory. Also be sure to always have copies of the directory available to hand out to new women.

When new women have filled out forms, photocopy the completed forms, and bring the copies and a three-hole punch to the next meeting so that all the women there can add the new women's forms to their own directory.

IDEA 32
picture directory

Take a picture of every woman in your ministry. A Polaroid camera or a digital camera will make the picture taking easy.

Mount the pictures on poster board, and write each woman's name underneath her photo. Display the sheets of poster board on the wall or prop them up on easels at every women's ministry function. This is a great way to help people put names with faces.

When a new woman has come to several events, ask her if she'd like to add her picture to the gallery to help the other women get to know her better.

Women's Ministry Directory

Name: _____

Address: _____

_____

Phone number: _____

E-mail address: _____

Birthday: _____

Anniversary: _____

Family or roomates (include names, ages, relationships, and birthdays when

appropriate)_____

_____

_____

_____

_____

During the week, I fill my days by_____

_____

_____

My favorite things to do for fun are _____

_____

I'm really good at _____

I like to serve by _____

My favorite colors are _____

My favorite foods are _____

I love to collect _____

I started coming to this church (year)_____

My favorite thing about this church is _____

My favorite Bible verses are _____

What would you like to tell the rest of group about yourself?

_____

_____

_____

_____

_____

IDEA 33
going places

You may find that there are a number of women in your church who sit at home week after week because they don't have anyone to do fun things with.

Form a Going Places group for those women. Survey the women in your group to find out what they're interested in doing. Then put a small group of women in charge of finding fun events, such as plays, concerts, museum tours, sporting events, citywide festivals, races, and more. Some women might also enjoy outdoor events such as hiking, boating, skiing, snowshoeing, or volleyball.

Put together a calendar of events that would be interesting to the group. Find one woman per event to take over the planning and coordinating responsibilities so that no one gets stuck with doing all the planning. Have the event planner/coordinator be responsible for getting out information about the event and coordinating transportation.

Depending on the size of your group, you may want to offer weekly events or monthly events. Be sure these events don't conflict with the women's ministry events you've planned.

IDEA 34
farewell affirmations

This is a great idea to use at the end of a retreat.

Tape a sheet of paper to each woman's back. Give each woman a pen that won't bleed through the paper. Encourage the women to mingle throughout the room and write little notes of affirmation on one another's papers.

This activity is a lot of fun because it takes a bit of coordination to write on someone else's paper while someone is writing on your own paper. Plus, there's a bit of mystery involved because you don't know what people are writing to you.

Have the women write notes to as many women as possible. In a group of ten to fifteen women, a fifteen-minute time frame should give everyone enough time to write a note to every other person in the room. In a group of more than fifteen women, fifteen minutes won't be enough time to get to everyone, but the women should write as many notes as they can.

When you call time, encourage women to return to their seats and take a few moments to read what others have written to them.✿

serving
OTHERS

Service is not a new concept to women—the quintessential nurturers in our world. Women take care of their husbands, their children, their parents, their in-laws, their siblings, their bosses, and their church's missionaries. Women are the ones who send thank-you cards, birthday cards, and Christmas cards. They're the ones who comfort the sick and sooth the frightened. Women are the ones who stay up until midnight to make cupcakes for school the next day, even though the child never thought to mention needing cupcakes until bedtime. Women are often selfless and tireless in their work for others. When they've organized themselves well, women have done incredible service for the poor, the sick, and the addicted. Women are truly the ones who care for the world.

But that doesn't mean there isn't room for improvement!

Service projects are a powerful tool in the women's ministry toolbox of ideas. Service projects help women fulfill the biblical call to love and serve others. At the same time, service projects help women learn to love God more and grow in their relationship with Jesus. Serving helps women love people more and see them as God's precious creations. Many women struggle with personal discontentment and discouragement. Service performed with the right motivation is the most effective way to battle dissatisfaction and resentment.

As powerful as service projects can be, they are too often a neglected part of women's ministry programs. And that's understandable. Women's ministry leaders are well aware that women work hard to serve others in their everyday lives. Churches often feel very strongly the calling to serve tired, spiritually hungry women, to give them respite and to build up their reserves. Women's ministry leaders want to reach women for Christ—to help them find a relationship with Jesus and grow in their knowledge of him. Many groups focus their efforts on events that will bring people to the church and either introduce them to Christ or encourage them in their relationship with Christ.

That's great! But there's so much more!

All Christian women should be actively involved in service. The Bible never calls for us to be spectators or, worse, to be needy creatures who continually enjoy being served without ever returning the favor by serving others. In fact, the Bible makes it quite clear that each Christian has been given a gift and is expected to use that gift for the benefit of the body.

Of course, it often happens that, while dozens or even hundreds may attend the banquets and the teas and even the Bible studies, only a very few will show up for a service project. Frankly, it can be hard to continue to plan service projects when no one seems to be interested.

Please, don't let that stop you.

In all of your teaching, in each of your events, urge every woman to serve others—to make a difference in someone else's life. Teach from the good examples of biblical women such as Rahab, Deborah, Abigail, Esther, and Mary. Strive to help women understand that serving the body of Christ and serving the world in Christ's service are not options. God has created each one of us to be active in our faith. And not one of us will be completely within God's will until we're exercising the gifts and talents he's given us.

Develop a core, even if it's only a few women, of eager servants. Have these women tell of the delightful benefits of serving God. Help their enthusiasm for helping people rub off on other women. And continue to encourage women to get involved. Make service part of your key goals for ministry to women. Consider making it a requirement that every leader within the women's ministry program must be involved in at least one service project per quarter. Constantly make women aware of all the opportunities for service in your church and your community.

The hidden benefit of service is that the rewards of serving others are far greater than the cost. The women in your church should be exposed to both the wonderful growth opportunities service provides and the wonderful rewards service brings.

IDEA 1
free haircuts

If you have hairstylists or beauticians in your women's group, encourage them to be involved in this easy service project.

Plan one night a month or quarter to spend an evening at your local homeless shelter giving the women and children free haircuts. You could also go to a local jail or shelter for battered women.

Encourage the hairstylists to chat with the women they're serving and to pray with them and talk about their faith. You may want to take some time before going to the shelter to train the hairstylists how to share Christ with someone. (See page 192 for training ideas.)

IDEA 2
date night with baby-sitting

Have the single women in your church provide free child care so that couples can enjoy a monthly date night at the church.

For the date night, create a coffeehouse atmosphere. Decorate tables with fresh flowers from the grocery store. Provide an assortment of desserts and coffee drinks, and have music groups from the church provide quiet background music. Encourage couples to come and enjoy an evening of conversation with each other or a time of fellowship with others.

The single women can provide care for infants as well as for children up to age twelve. At the end of the evening (a two-hour time frame is sufficient), allow the single women to take home the leftover desserts and the centerpieces from the tables.

IDEA 3
homeless shelter meals

Arrange with your local homeless shelter to provide the evening meal once a month. At some shelters, you can sign up to prepare and serve dinner on a particular day each month: for example, the third Sunday evening of the month. Some shelters only ask that you show up on the assigned day, and the shelter takes care of the planning and shopping and might even direct the cooking. For other shelters, you'll need to meet ahead of time to plan the meal you'll cook and to arrange for the shopping. Make sure you understand the policies of the shelter in your area and be sure to abide by all of their rules.

This service project is especially gratifying for women who learned to cook for large families or who have worked in school cafeterias. This is a wonderful opportunity for them to use their unique abilities. It's also a great way to serve outside the church. Many churches have groups that have served at homeless shelters on a regular basis for several years.

IDEA 4
eco-ladies

Form a group of environmentally responsible women from your church to develop an ecologically sound way to dispose of and recycle all of the paper and plastic waste from your church.

Have the group meet to come up with short- and long-term stewardship goals for this program. For example, the group may find ways to buy more earth-friendly products, such as recycled paper goods and cleaners that are less toxic to the environment and people than the ones the church has been using. The group might also explore cost-saving measures and recycling options. For example, it may be as easy as providing recycling bins for paper scraps and for plastic waste near the location of the church supplies. Have the group work with the church staff to monitor the church's needs and to suggest ways the church can be a better steward of its money and take better care of the world.

These women could also explore ways that individuals can be better stewards of their resources at home and then develop presentations to make to the women in your church.

With careful planning, your group can help the church make wise purchases that will save money and create less waste.

IDEA 5
clothing giveaway

This service project can benefit women inside and outside your church, and it's a great outreach event.

For several weeks prior to your event, ask women in your church to donate seasonally appropriate used clothing and linens in good condition. You can either limit your request to women's clothing or include children's clothing and men's clothing as well.

Several days before the event, you'll need to organize a team of volunteers to sort the clothing by gender, size, and type and to organize all the items on tables and racks. Anything not appropriate can be discarded.

Have another team of volunteers work on the day of the exchange to keep everything in order, help people find the right sizes, put selected clothing in bags, and direct indoor traffic. You'll need to decide whether you want to charge money for the clothing or give the clothing away. If you do charge money, donate the money to a local charity.

Invite everyone from your church to attend the exchange. Keep the exchange closed to the public, but do allow church members to bring anyone they want with them. This way, community people who come will have at least one personal connection to the church, and your church members may feel more comfortable inviting them to other church functions and explaining the ministries of the church to them.

You'll need a third team of women to "tear down" the event, packing the leftover clothes to give to a Christian charity, putting tables away, and cleaning the area.

IDEA 6
purse exchange

As part of another women's ministry meeting, have all the women bring all of the unwanted purses they have in their closets. Display the purses on tables around the room. At the end of the meeting, invite the women to take a couple of purses home with them.

IDEA 7
abun*dance* troupe

Form a dance ministry for the women in your church who are trained in dance and theater. The dance group can provide special programs for women's ministry events, worship services, and for community events such as parades and festivals. The group may want to create short skits, sacred dance routines, and mime.

IDEA 8
mission sewing

Form a sewing group to serve a particular population within your community. For example, you might want to serve migrant farm-workers or teenage mothers in your area. Encourage the women to meet weekly at a woman's home. The women can refurbish clothing (mending tears and replacing buttons) on donated clothing. They can also make children's clothing and machine quilts from scraps of fabric. In the winter, women might knit and crochet hats, mittens, and scarves. To raise funds for the supplies they need, the women could sell some of the items they make to the church congregation. At least once a season or once a month, deliver the items to the regional charity that serves the migrant workers, teenage moms, or other group you've chosen to serve.

IDEA 9
church murals

Decorate the walls of your church with these unique murals. Give each woman a 6x6-inch square of canvas. Choose a color theme and a subject theme. For example, perhaps you want to decorate in shades of green and lavender, and perhaps you'd like to decorate around the theme of Faith, Hope, and Love. Provide paint, brushes, and any other necessary art supplies. Allow women to apply the paint to the canvas however they see fit. Some women may want to use a brush; others may want to spatter the paint or use their fingers.

When the squares are finished, fit them into large wall frames, and put them up around the room. You'll end up with large wall paintings that have a patchwork effect. This project gives women the opportunity to use their gifts as a form of worship, and their creativity will bless the entire congregation of your church.

IDEA 10
student helpers

In one church, several of the young women were being trained in nursing or EMT programs while a number of older women in the church were in need of assistance and were considering moving to assisted-living homes or nursing homes. The church developed a program that paired the young nursing students with the older women. The young women moved into the older women's homes and cared for them, which meant that the young women received free housing, as well as practical training for their career. The older women received care, help with chores, and company. The families of both the college women and the senior women also participated in the process and ensured a high level of accountability.

Other churches could adopt a similar program, or they could develop programs to pair women with other skills with those who could benefit from those skills.

IDEA 11
thanksgiving baskets

Each year, your women's ministry can provide Thanksgiving baskets for church families. Meet with your leadership team to talk about which families you need to help and how many families you can help. Don't make the names of the families public information. You may choose to help a family that has struggled for a long time, one with a new baby or an illness, the family of someone who has lost his or her job, or a single person.

Most families that need help need more than just a one-day celebration meal, so consider providing

• a complete Thanksgiving dinner with all the ingredients necessary for preparing the dinner. (Tuck in some favorite recipes from the women in the congregation.)

• a week's supply of groceries, including paper towels, toilet paper, diapers (if necessary), cereal, milk, eggs, bread, meat, and canned goods.

• a pantry pack with staples such as flour, sugar, salt, spices, peanut butter, macaroni and cheese, and tuna.

When possible, tailor these baskets according to the size and preferences of the families.

You'll find year after year that the biggest fans of the program are those who received baskets in previous years. Those who received them in the past will be excited about helping prepare these baskets for others.

In mid-October, announce the program in your church's bulletin. Begin gathering names. Also begin gathering donations for the baskets, including meat certificates from the local grocery store, gift cards from local discount stores, sacks of canned goods, and whatever women feel led to provide.

Deliver the baskets the second week of November.

IDEA 12
evangelube

At least once a year, arrange a free oil-change service for the single moms in your congregation or in the neighborhood surrounding your church. The women's ministry should provide the oil and filters, as well as windshield wipers and brake and transmission fluids. The women's ministry should also organize and advertise the event.

Work with the men's ministry program in your church to find volunteers to do the labor. Work with the church's youth ministry program to find volunteers to provide car washes and simple detailing work too.

Hold the event on a Saturday in early fall before the weather gets cold. Encourage the men to point out any problems (such as bald tires or bad brakes) they might notice when they change the oil.

You'll find that this service promotes unity, fellowship, and community among the members of your congregation. It's also a fantastic outreach to the neighborhood.

IDEA 13
christmas eve staff buffet

Christmas Eve can be a busy time for the staff of a church. Multiple services can mean that the pastoral staff works the entire day in preparation and then late into the evening at the services.

Your women's ministry can serve your church's staff by providing a buffet for them and their families on Christmas Eve. Send elegant invitations to each pastor and his family. Set up the buffet mid-afternoon. The buffet can be as easy as a potluck provided by the women of your church. Provide a team of women to set up and maintain the buffet and to tear it down and clean up afterward.

The buffet arrangement allows the pastors and other staff to grab a bite to eat anytime during the afternoon and evening. It also provides a time for them to connect with their families on a very busy day.

IDEA 14
mitten ministry

Women who are incarcerated often have very little family nearby and no support system. When they are released from prison or when they are part of a work release program, they often must wait for a bus because they have no other transportation. These women may not have appropriate clothing for standing outside in cold weather.

Your women's ministry can provide mittens, hats, and scarves for these women. Invite women to donate good-quality items. With a little investigation, you may be able to find a source that would sell you these items at cost.

Have women "hang out" at bus stops with pockets stuffed with extra mittens and gloves that they can offer to women who need them.

Not only will women have an opportunity to share a little warmth; they'll also have an opportunity to share the hope of the gospel with these women.

IDEA 15
cell-group baby-sitting

Many churches have small Bible study groups that meet throughout the week. For families with children, hiring a sitter every week can be expensive. Set up a network of baby-sitters for each night that your church has small-group meetings. Setting up the network can be as easy as helping parents trade nights of child care.

You may want to have children go to a couple's house or gather at the church. Or have teens provide free baby-sitting while their own parents are at the same cell meeting. Another idea is to coordinate with the children's ministry program in your church to have the kids meet for their own small-group Bible study.

Be sure to think of all safety issues! Provide accountability by having two responsible people in charge of the children. The two people should be of opposite gender, and they should not be related or married.

Parents who participate can use a phone tree or e-mail to keep in touch, though it's helpful if one person or group coordinates the effort.

Not only do these baby-sitting arrangements give parents peace of mind, but they also help the children in your church get to know one another better.

IDEA 16
soup mixes

You can use these soup mixes in a variety of ways. You might use them as fundraisers by selling the mixes at craft shows or festivals. You can give them away as gifts to visitors at your church or distribute them in your church's neighborhood as an outreach project. You can also have the women in your church make them as simple, inexpensive holiday gifts for their own family and friends.

Savory Bean Soup (makes 12 gifts)
12 pint-size Mason jars
4 cups dried black beans
4 cups great northern beans
4 cups red kidney beans
4 cups pinto beans
4 cups green split peas
4 cups yellow split peas

Layer one-third cup of each kind of bean in a wide-mouth pint jar to make pretty layers. Put the following spices in a small plastic sandwich bag. (The following ingredient list is for each jar. You'll need to make twelve packets and put one packet in each jar.) Cut squares of pretty fabric with pinking shears, and place the fabric squares on top of the lids before screwing on the rings.

Savory Bean Soup Seasonings
3 teaspoons beef bouillon
3 tablespoons dried chives
1 teaspoon dried savory
½ teaspoon pepper
1 bay leaf

Photocopy the directions on page 48, and attach one copy to each jar.

Creamy Potato Soup (makes 4 gifts)
4 pint-size Mason jars
3 ⅓ cups dried potato flakes
2 ½ cups dried milk powder
½ cup powdered coffee creamer
4 tablespoons chicken bouillon
4 teaspoons dried minced onion
2 teaspoons dried parsley
½ teaspoon white pepper
½ teaspoon dried thyme
3 teaspoons salt

Mix in a large mixing bowl with a wire whisk. Divide the mix between four pint jars. Cut squares of pretty fabric with pinking shears, and place the fabric on the lids before screwing on the rings.

Photocopy the instructions on page 49, and attach to the jars with pretty ribbons.

IDEA 17
widows luncheon or tea

At least once a year, host a luncheon or tea that caters to the widows in your church. Provide elegant food and a small, prettily wrapped gift for each lady. Serve the meal on china, and use lace or fabric tablecloths and napkins. If your church doesn't have these items,

Savory Bean Soup

Set aside the seasoning packet.

Put the beans in a large pot with 9 cups of water. Bring the beans and water to a boil and boil for 3 minutes. Set aside for an hour.

Drain and rinse the beans. Add 5 cups of water and the seasoning packet to the beans and cook for 1 1/2 hours. Add 1 can of diced tomatoes and a teaspoon of salt. Simmer for 20 minutes. Take out the bay leaf.

Enjoy!

Savory Bean Soup

Set aside the seasoning packet.

Put the beans in a large pot with 9 cups of water. Bring the beans and water to a boil and boil for 3 minutes. Set aside for an hour.

Drain and rinse the beans. Add 5 cups of water and the seasoning packet to the beans and cook for 1 1/2 hours. Add 1 can of diced tomatoes and a teaspoon of salt. Simmer for 20 minutes. Take out the bay leaf.

Enjoy!

Creamy Potato Soup

Mix ½ cup of the dry mix with 1 cup of boiling water. Stir until smooth and creamy.

Yum!

Creamy Potato Soup

Mix ½ cup of the dry mix with 1 cup of boiling water. Stir until smooth and creamy.

Yum!

Creamy Potato Soup

Mix ½ cup of the dry mix with 1 cup of boiling water. Stir until smooth and creamy.

Yum!

have younger women in your church bring enough linens and china to set one table each. Have the younger women, teenagers, and girls in the church serve and provide special music.

IDEA 18
service brochure

As ministry coordinators, it's easy to focus on providing studies and events that will help women grow spiritually. It's harder to provide opportunities that will get women involved in ministry themselves.

Be purposeful about contacting the other areas in the church and asking them how the women in the church can minister to others.

Regularly publish a listing of ways women can volunteer to serve in the church. Encourage service as a vital way to grow spiritually.

IDEA 19
mothers' helpers

Many times, young mothers are overwhelmed with taking care of their children and their homes, while older women may not have enough to occupy their days. Serve both needs by organizing the older women into a group of mothers' helpers.

The older women can help by taking care of the children for a couple of hours to give the young women a chance to enjoy a couple hours of quiet or to run errands. Some older women might also enjoy preparing a meal in exchange for the opportunity to spend an evening with a family.

Talk with the older women first to find out what their skills are and how much time they'd be willing to serve. Then talk with the young moms to find out what their needs are. Match the women up, and encourage them to get together on a regular basis.

IDEA 20
home-project teams

Some projects, including painting, wallpapering, and landscaping, are more fun when others pitch in and help.

Find out what the women in your group like to do. Then organize the women into project teams.

In your women's ministry newsletter or brochure, list the jobs your project teams are willing to tackle. Include a phone number or e-mail address for each team so that a woman who needs help with a project can contact the right team.

These teams can also serve the community. Community groups may organize paintathons or yardwork days for the elderly. In fact, your women's ministry could organize such an event. Work with a community agency to find people who would benefit from your group's help.

IDEA 21
after-school care

Stay-at-home moms could offer a vital service to work-away-from-home moms by offering after-school care for their children in your church. The after-school care would give stay-at-home moms a chance to serve and a chance to get to know the other women in the church. The project could also provide huge financial help to working moms.

This idea works especially well if your church is within walking distance to an elementary school or middle school.

Form rotating teams of moms or retired women who would enjoy watching children at your church building after school. Have the women serve for a week at a time.

The women should arrive at the elementary school five minutes before school lets out and walk the children to the church building. Older children can walk by themselves. It should be very clear, though, which children are expected to come to the church after school so that caregivers can take attendance and make sure all the kids who are expected to be there arrive safely.

At the church, the women can provide a simple snack and provide a quiet room with tables, pencils, calculators, and other supplies so kids can do their homework. They can have board games available and can also organize group games such as basketball or kickball.

Be sure to check with the children's ministry team to make sure that you've accounted for all liability and safety issues. In fact, you may want to coordinate this project with the children's minister at your church.

Make sure the moms know when they must pick up their children. For example, you might want to say that all children must be picked up by 5:30. This way the helpers can get back to their own homes at a reasonable hour.

You can easily turn this into an outreach project by inviting children who don't usually come to your church to come to the after-school program. Then provide their moms with information about your women's ministry program and offer them a friendly, personal invitation to come.

IDEA 22
unseen helpers

Some women love to serve behind the scenes. In fact, they steer clear of projects that would call attention to themselves.

These women may truly enjoy big cleaning or organizing projects. Talk to the other ministry leaders in your church to find out what needs to be done. For example, perhaps the music library needs to be organized; all the church's Bible times costumes may need to be cleaned, mended, and organized by size; all the church's woodwork needs to be cleaned and polished; or the children's ministry supply closet needs to be cataloged and organized.

Make the women in your group aware of these opportunities to serve. For each project, appoint an organizer who can gather a small group of women to take care of the need.

You may even want to put together an all-Saturday organizing party. Encourage the women to bring a sack lunch and donate a day of work to the church. It will help the church be a better steward of its resources.

IDEA 23
music lessons

Are there women in your church who are gifted musicians? Some would welcome opportunities to share their skills with others. And there are many children who would benefit from learning to play an instrument. But music lessons are expensive, and some families just can't afford them.

Encourage the musically gifted women in your church to offer free music lessons to the kids in your church as a service project. Each teacher could donate one or two hours a week to teach up to four children.

This project benefits everyone involved. The children will benefit from learning music. The teachers will benefit from the opportunity to serve. And the parents will benefit financially. What's more, everyone will benefit from a greater sense of community. The church can offer the space for the lessons.

Encourage all of the music teachers to incorporate sacred music into their lessons so that the children learn to appreciate the musical heritage of the church. If it's appropriate in your church, the children can eventually provide music for offertories during worship services.

If free lessons aren't an option, the women might offer lessons at a reduced fee or charge the going rate for the music lessons and donate a portion of the fee to a missions project.

IDEA 24
life-skills classes

Like-skills classes offer a great opportunity to help the troubled teens in your community.

Offer a series of these classes to the teens at your local alternative high school. Be sure to work in partnership with the school!

Find women in your church who can teach such skills as balancing a checkbook, living on a budget, cooking nutritious and low-cost meals, basic child care, saving money, dressing for the work world, basic sewing and mending, and interviewing for a job.

You can offer the classes either at your church building or at the school.

The teachers can use this opportunity not only to teach young women life skills, but also to be warm, friendly, loving, Christ-like examples.

IDEA 25
emergency prayer partners

Many women truly enjoy praying for others. Send these women out in groups of two or three to pray in hospital emergency rooms. Be sure to get permission from the hospital authorities first. You may want to coordinate your efforts with the hospital chaplain or pastor.

The women can sit and pray silently for those who come into the emergency room. If it's appropriate, and if it's allowed by the hospital, they can gently approach people and ask if they can pray for them or with them.

Encourage the women to be respectful, gentle, and polite.

Before sending the women out, you may want to talk with them about how to share Christ with others and how to handle emergency situations with grace. Talk about what would be appropriate or inappropriate for them to pray for as they pray with people who may not be Christians.

IDEA 26
fundraising meals

Use these low-cost meals to raise money for service projects or missions work. You can charge five dollars for any of these meals. Your costs will easily be taken care of, but if the women in your church donate the ingredients, your profit margin will be much higher.

• **Baked Potato Bar.** Buy potatoes in fifty-pound bags from your local supermarket. Wash the potatoes, rub them with oil, pierce them with a fork, and wrap them with foil before baking for about an hour in a preheated oven. Have the women in your church donate toppings, including butter, sour cream, bacon bits, chives, chili, cooked broccoli, cheese, sautéed mushrooms, barbecued beef, and whatever else you think would be good. Provide beverages and homemade cookies and brownies. Plan on two potatoes per person.

• **Beans and Ham Supper.** Have several women in the group use Crock-Pot electric cookers to make ham and beans. Here's a basic recipe. Soak a two-pound bag of white great northern beans overnight the night before the event. The morning of the event, drain the beans and place them in a Crock-Pot. Add fresh water until the beans are covered by two to three inches of water. Add one chopped onion and one to two cups of ham chopped in small pieces. Cook the beans all day, checking to make sure there's enough water so that the beans don't scorch. Start the beans on high and turn to low if needed. Add salt to taste when the beans are tender and the skins are bursting. Serve the beans with cornbread. Provide ketchup, mustard, and relish for the beans and butter for the cornbread. Provide homemade desserts also. Pie is especially good with this supper.

• **Chicken and Noodles Dinner.** Have several women in the group make Crock-Pots of chicken and noodles. Other women can make mashed potatoes. Here's a basic recipe for chicken and noodles. Boil a small chicken on top of the stove for several hours. Remove the chicken from the broth. Cool the chicken and the broth. Remove the meat from the bones, and chop the meat into small pieces. Skim the fat from the broth and discard the fat. Add the chicken meat to the broth and heat both in a Crock-Pot. Season the chicken broth with salt and pepper and a little chicken bouillon, if you desire. Add water if needed to fill the Crock-Pot. Half an hour before serving, add one package of frozen egg noodles. Provide bowls. Put a scoop of mashed potatoes in each bowl, and serve the chicken and noodles over the top. Serve with homemade desserts.

• **Chili Cook-Off.** Have several women bring a Crock-Pot of their favorite homemade chili. Have other women bring crackers, hot sauce, and cornbread or rolls. Set up the Crock-Pots around the room, and have each "chef" serve small portions of her chili in insulated cups so that the guests will be able to sample several different kinds of chili. Serve with homemade desserts.

IDEA 27
spiritual friends

Help the young women in your church grow to love Christ and to live their lives devoted to him. Each year, match up one adult woman with a young girl from your church.

You can do this project with seventh-, eighth-, or ninth-grade girls. Have the friends meet once a month to do something fun (have ice cream, go bowling, go hiking, go to tea) and to talk about school, boys, family, and spiritual things. Some women and girls may want to do a formal Bible study together.

At the end of the year, hold a banquet for the women and girls. Have the adult women, one by one, tell the rest of the group about the girl she's been friends with all year and how the girl has grown in

Christ. Have each woman present an inspirational Christian book to the girl. Then have the woman honor the girl by praying for her in front of the group.

IDEA 28
errand runners

Honor the older adults in your congregation by helping them with the errands they need to run. Make a list of older adults who could use a hand now and then. Make another list of women who could help.

Have each available woman take responsibility for one or two older adults. Encourage the women to build friendships with the older adults by calling them on the phone once or twice a week to check in with them and by offering help with rides or errands. Also encourage the women to invite the older adults into their own homes for meals or holiday celebrations.

IDEA 29
college student connection

The years away at college can be hard on a young adult's faith and pocketbook. The women in your church can help.

Keep an address list of all the college kids from your church. At least twice a semester, have the women in your church put together care packages to send to them. The packages might include these items:

- rolls of quarters for laundry
- fast-food coupons
- coffeehouse gift certificates
- home-baked cookies and brownies
- encouraging cards and letters
- church newsletters or bulletins
- copies of the local paper with interesting stories about people they know
- packets of hot chocolate and a fun mug
- a devotional book or Bible

It would also be a great idea to keep a list of all the college kids' e-mail addresses and to have the women send frequent, encouraging e-mails to them.

IDEA 30
missionary visits

Being on furlough can be very stressful for missionaries. Here are some great ways the women in your church can help them make the most of their time in the States.

• **Housing.** Missionaries often find themselves shuttled from one spare bedroom to another during their stay. This arrangement is very difficult for families. Find out if there are women in your congregation who live somewhere else during the summer or winter and have homes where missionaries could stay for several weeks or months. Another option is to find women who have mother-in-law apartments in their basements or over their garages. Still another idea is to raise funds to convert someone's garage or backyard cottage into missionary housing or to buy an inexpensive home and maintain it (with the other churches in your area) for all the missionaries who visit your community.

• **Supplies.** Missionaries often collect a lot of resources and supplies during a stay in the States, and a lot of it is donated by churches. Getting all of that material back to the country where they serve can be very expensive. Raise the money to ship all of the supplies to the countries where the missionaries serve so that they don't have to take extra packages on the plane. Take care of the packing and the shipping so the missionaries don't have to deal with the details.

• **Transportation.** Missionaries have lots of errands to run and people to see during their short time in the States. You can help them make the best use of their time by helping with transportation. Find women in your church who have extra vehicles they could spare for several weeks at a time, and make the vehicles available to the missionaries. Keep in mind that missionaries who come to the States with their children may need more than one vehicle at times.

• **Community Services.** Help missionaries find their way around town by providing a guide (with maps) to local services. For example, you may want to include information such as:

+ local parks and recreation centers
+ directions to the post office
+ the best local restaurants
+ the location of ethnic grocery stores
+ directions to libraries

+ directions to copy centers

+ directions to Christian bookstores

+ directions to the best shopping centers

• **Recreation.** Missionaries and their families have to be "on" a lot during their stays here. Many times their families desperately need some private, downtime to rest. Collect videos or DVDs for the families to watch during their stay. Collect good books and magazines that families may have missed during their time overseas. You may also want to provide temporary memberships at health clubs and recreation centers.

• **Presentation Time.** Make your women's ministry events open to missionaries who would like to make presentations to your group. Many missionaries spend much of their furlough educating churches about their ministry and raising support for the field. Prepare the women in your church for a missionary's presentation by making them aware of the great work missionaries do around the world. To make the most of the missionary's time, encourage the women to be generous and to give sacrificially to missionaries so that the gospel of Christ is spread around the world.

IDEA 31
sunday morning doughnuts

Raise money for service projects by selling coffee, hot chocolate, and doughnuts or sweet rolls on Sunday mornings.

If the women in your group make the rolls or donate the doughnuts, your profit margin will be much higher.

In some churches, it works well to have church members bring in all of their unwanted coffee mugs. The coffee mugs cut down on the amount of money spent on paper goods. Find a cart on which to store the mugs. Each week, assign volunteers to the tasks of bringing the food, making the coffee, and washing the mugs after church.

IDEA 32
crisis-pregnancy help

Help the young women in your community who are coping with crisis pregnancies.

Contact the local crisis pregnancy center to find out what supplies the center needs. Then host a baby shower to provide the center with all those items. Invite all the women in your church to come. Make the list of supplies available ahead of time, and encourage women to purchase the items and bring them to the baby shower. Have the women bring their purchased items (there's no need to wrap them) to the shower and put the items on display tables.

Use baby shower decorations for the party. At the shower, give the women time to view all of the donated items. Then enjoy baby-shower food; for example, serve a decorated cake, punch, mints, and nuts. Invite a woman from the crisis-pregnancy center to give a presentation about the young women who are served by the organization. Then break up into small groups of three or four to pray specifically for the center, the pregnant women, and the babies they will have.

Some women may want to do more. Encourage them to volunteer to help at the center. Other women may volunteer to host a pregnant girl in their homes while she awaits the birth of her baby.✿

spiritual GROWTH

Spiritual growth must be the heart of every women's ministry program. Our ultimate goal is to help women love Jesus Christ with their whole hearts and to live their lives in passionate devotion and service to him.

The ideas in this section will help the women in your church love Jesus more. To love Jesus, women need to spend time with him in prayer. Jesus wants a relationship with us, and that takes time. Provide lots of opportunities for the women at your church to get to know the God they serve.

Study is important too. We must understand what Scripture says about our God and about having faith in him. Scripture study is so important in today's world because there are so many misconceptions floating around. Use the activities in this section to help women dig into their God-inspired Bibles to learn about their Lord.

It's also helpful for women to spend time with other women who know and love Jesus. In every church, there are women who are wise and spiritually mature. These women are great examples to the others. Spiritually mature women can encourage others, inspire others, instruct others, counsel others, and gently rebuke others when needed. There is much that women can learn from one another.

Build your program around spiritual growth activities and Bible study, but be sure to balance these activities with fellowship and celebration.

IDEA 1
mentoring program

 Every women's ministry can benefit from a mentoring program.

The first step is to look for women in your church who have the ability to encourage others in their spiritual walk. It will be natural to look for older women who have been Christians for a number of years and who have gained spiritual wisdom and maturity, but don't neglect women in their thirties and forties who love God and want to encourage other women.

Next, look for women in their teens, twenties, and thirties who would be interested in meeting with a mentor. Also consider older women who are new in their relationships with Jesus.

Be sure to meet with the mentors to explain your expectations and guidelines for mentoring. Then, with a great deal of prayer, match each participating woman with a mentor.

Have the pairs sign a statement that lists out the specifics of the relationship. Here are some ideas:

• **Stay in touch with e-mail or snail-mail at least once a week.** The weekly communication should provide encouragement and help to develop a sincere friendship.

• **Meet at least once every other week to talk about spiritual growth issues.** It's important that a mentor relationship stay focused on spiritual growth. Encourage mentors to talk with the women they're mentoring about where they'd like to grow in their relationship with Christ. Have each pair make a list of growth areas. Each time the women meet, they can talk about a different area of growth. The mentor might suggest books they can read together. Some pairs might want to go through a Bible study together. There are many small-group Bible studies available that can be adapted easily to a two-person group.

- **Keep the mentor connection active for at least one semester.** It takes awhile for people to know each other well. Encourage pairs to work on their relationship for at least three or four months. Be aware, though, that there might be some relationships that just don't work out. Be prepared to reassign people if pairs don't click or if problems come up. At the end of the time period people have agreed to, be sure to allow people to end the relationship gracefully or to sign up for another semester.

- **Attend at least one women's ministry event together, and do one service project together.** Keeping women connected to your program will ensure they don't become isolated and go off on tangents. Doing service projects together will help prevent women becoming too self-focused.

- **Have fun together!** The women should enjoy their time together and get together sometimes just for fun. Encourage the women to nurture their friendship even after the mentoring partnership ends.

The mentors will be able to help young women get plugged into the church and become grounded in their relationship with God.

IDEA 2
campus Bible study

Begin an outreach to the college women in your area by starting several small-group Bible studies. Encourage several of your church's college-age women to meet for Bible study at the university's student-union food court during mealtimes. This location and time will make the group easy to find and less threatening for new Christians. The group will also be visible to non-Christians who may approach the group out of curiosity and express interest in joining.

Encourage the group to study a theme of a particular Bible book for the entire semester. You'll need at least one leader who can commit to come each week, but allow the groups to be open and flexible to encourage women to drop by whenever possible and to welcome newcomers.

Advertise the Bible studies by posting fliers around campus and in the dorms. Be sure to invite young career-age women from your church too. Not only does this Bible study give young women a chance to study the Bible, but it also gives them an easy way to be bold about their faith in a non-Christian setting. And through their Bible study, college women will develop an on-campus network of Christian friends to turn to for friendship and support.

IDEA 3
women's library

Gather a compact library of Christian books for women in your church. Even if your church has a general library, you may want to collect materials that deal specifically with women's issues. You can house your library in a rolling cart, which would be available at all your women's ministry events, or in an out-of-the-way closet. Encourage women to donate nonfiction Christian books they have found helpful. Include books on Christian living, reference books, Bible study books, different Bible translations, and other helpful resources. Include a self-service check-out station, book reviews of current popular Christian reading, and a book wish list. If necessary, staff the library with rotating volunteers from the women's ministry. Form a review board in case there is ever a question about a book's suitability. If you have more books than you need, pack them up and send them to missionaries overseas.

IDEA 4
coffeehouse meetings

Chances are the coffeehouses in your town that are bustling in the evenings are nearly empty during the day. These places can provide quiet places for your church's weekday women's ministry Bible studies. You may want to arrange to pay the coffeehouse a small fee to ensure that you have a section of the coffeehouse reserved each week for your meetings. Be sure to encourage the women to purchase beverages and snacks from the coffeehouse too. You may be able to work out a deal with the owner for a special discount for your group. You may also want to encourage the women in your group to meet at the coffeehouse on their own or with one or two friends during the week for fellowship and prayer.

IDEA 5
gathering time

A gathering time works great if women come for Bible study at the church and then meet in small groups throughout the church.

Have all the groups gather together for praise and worship during the first half-hour of your time together. Find someone to lead the singing and prayer. Each week, invite one woman to share how God has worked in her life and how she came to know and love God.

The gathering time is a great way to foster a sense of community in your group. It also gives women an opportunity to be encouraged by someone else's walk with God. The sharing time helps women guard against "judging by appearances" and assuming that everyone else has always led a "perfect" Christian life. The women in your group will be amazed at the circumstances God has brought each woman through, the lessons he has taught along the way, and his consistent, perfect faithfulness.

IDEA 6
prayer groups

Encourage small groups of women to meet together simply to pray. Prayer groups work best if there is nothing else on the agenda for the meeting. As soon as the women arrive, they should begin to pray, and they should pray until the meeting time is over.

A prepared list of prayer concerns works well. Find someone to be responsible for gathering prayer concerns ahead of time, including global concerns, local concerns, church concerns, and the personal struggles of the people from the women's ministry. She should print the list, copy it, and hand a list to each woman as she arrives. Prepared lists save the time it would take to gather requests or to tell everyone about the concerns before prayer begins. Encourage the women to pray from the prayer list as they feel led by God and to add their own concerns.

It also helps if someone sets an alarm so the women know when the prayer time is finished. Knowing the alarm is set will allow women in the group to focus all their attention on prayer.

Once prayer time is over, the women can chat and enjoy one another's company.

IDEA 7
journals

Journaling is a great way to facilitate spiritual growth.

Encourage the women in your group to journal by providing binders for each woman. Pass out packets of journaling sheets to be included in the binders. Have tabs available for such things as prayer, Bible study notes, and personal growth. Encourage the women to bring their journals to all meetings. Be sure to provide time to write in the journals during meetings.

IDEA 8
ten quiet-time reminders

Help the women in your group have a daily time with God by sending everyone a short e-mail each day with a Scripture passage to read, a question to ponder, and a short list of things to pray for. Here are some ideas to get you started. You can personalize by adding prayer requests from the members of your group.

• Read John 1:1-18. Who is Jesus and what has he done for you? Pray a prayer of thanksgiving, telling God all the reasons you're thankful for his Son.

• Read Philippians 4:4-9. What kind of attitude would you like to cultivate in your own life? How can you do this? Spend some time in prayer rejoicing in the Lord.

• Read Colossians 3:1-17. What kind of behavior is worthy of us as God's chosen people? What can you do to live up to this passage? Ask God to help you love others more.

• Read 1 Timothy 2:1-4. How can you incorporate the instructions in this passage into your regular prayer life? Take time right now to pray for those you know and for those in authority.

• Read 1 Timothy 6:6-10. Why is contentment so important, yet so difficult? What can you do to be more content? Right now, spend five full minutes thanking God for his blessings and gifts to you.

• Read 2 Timothy 2:3-7. How can you serve God with single-minded devotion? Talk to God right now about how you can spend your days serving him.

• Read Titus 3:3-8. How does embracing these truths help us devote ourselves to doing what is good? Meditate on God's kindness, love, and mercy. Praise God for his goodness to you.

• Read Hebrews 10:19-25. This is a great summary of what we're to be about as Christians. How would you summarize the Christian life? Draw near to God right now in prayer. Ask God to help you hold unswervingly to the faith, and ask God to help you consider how you can encourage others.

• Read James 1:1-8. How can you consider today's hardships as pure joy? How are today's hardships developing perseverance in you? Stop what you're doing right now, and ask God to give you the wisdom you need to face this day.

• Read 1 John 3:16-20. How can you, this very day, love someone else with actions and truth? Why is love so important for Christians? Pray, and ask God to increase your love for others and show you opportunities to act out your love today.

IDEA 9
journal in a jar

Create these journal gifts to give as gifts to the women in your congregation. They're inexpensive, quick to make, and suitable for any occasion, and they will help women in your church grow to love God more.

For each gift, you'll need a quart-size canning jar, a blank journal, a pretty pen, a square of calico fabric, pretty ribbon that coordinates with the fabric, and one photocopy of pages 68-72. If you want, add other things, such as small candies, tea bags, or a small devotional book.

To make each gift, photocopy pages 68-72 on pretty paper. Use a paper cutter to cut apart the slips. Fold the strips in half, and stuff them in the jar along with the pretty pen. Save the tag to tie to the jar. Next, use pinking shears to cut a square of fabric slightly bigger than the diameter of the jar's mouth. Put the fabric over the lid, and screw on the ring. Use the ribbon to tie the blank journal to the jar and attach the tag.

Journal in a Jar

Use this journal to explore your relationship with God in a very personal way. Take out one slip of paper, and read the question. Spend some time praying about the question. Then write your answer to the question in the journal.

Why did God create me?

What is my God-given purpose in life?

How has God shown his love for me?

What would I like my non-Christian friends to understand about why I love God?

What do my trials help me to know about God?

What do I find delightful about God?

What are my secret doubts about God?

What are my deepest fears? How can I overcome those?

What in this world breaks God's heart? Does it break my heart too?

How will I rejoice and be glad in this day that God has made?

How will I give myself as a living sacrifice to God?

What is worship? (Describe a time of sweet worship that affected you deeply.)

What are my favorite worship songs? (Find a quiet place and sing them to God. Explain why you love them.)

What does it mean to "be still and know that I am God"?
What do I know about God when I'm still?

What are my biggest questions about life,
God, and faith?

What does God's creation tell me about him?

What does God look like?

How does God answer my prayers? How does he
know what's best for me?

Do my prayers change what God plans to do?

Why has God made me the way I am, with my own
particular strengths and weakness?

Why did God give me the family that I have?

What does it mean to "act justly and to love mercy
and to walk humbly" with God?

How can I pray without ceasing?

Does my light truly shine, or have I hidden it under a basket?

I love God most when...

I doubt God most when...

I get angry with God when...

I know God is with me every moment because...

When I consider God's plan to save me through Jesus' death, I feel...

What do I appreciate most about the church I attend?

If I could change anything about the way the church operates, I would change...

Why did God create the church? What is church for?

What do I find the most troubling about the way
Christianity is lived today?

Why don't more people put their faith in God?

What is praiseworthy about God the Father?
God the Son? God the Holy Spirit?

What blessings has God given to me?

SEVEN TEN-MINUTE DEVOTIONS

There are lots of women's ministry programs, such as banquets, retreats, or even worship services, that need an added spiritual connection. These short devotions are perfect for those occasions. The activities work with any size group, they require few supplies, and they work with new Christians and experienced Christians alike.

If you're using these devotions with a large group, don't try to lead one mass discussion. Break up the large group into smaller groups of eight to ten. These devotions assume that women will be sitting around tables in small groups. If the women aren't already sitting at small tables, have them group themselves in groups of eight to ten. In some cases, you may need to provide a work surface or something to write on. Whether or not you need a work surface will be very clear in a quick reading of the devotion.

DEVOTION 1
lemon-aid

Set out bowls of lemons at each of the tables where the women will sit.

To begin the devotion, have each woman take a lemon and brainstorm together about all the different things lemons are used for. See which table can come up with the longest list.

SAY **You all came up with some pretty impressive lists of all the different things lemons can be used for. There's a common saying that goes like this: When life gives you lemons, make lemonade. That's pretty similar to a concept Paul taught in the book of Romans. Listen to this verse. "And we know that in all things God works for the good of those who love him, who have been called according to his purpose"** (Romans 8:28). **God is a master lemonade maker! At your table, talk about the times in your life God has brought something good out of bad situations.**

Give the women several minutes to talk, then gather their attention, and ask:

• **Why do you think bad things happen?**

• **When have you seen God make good come out of bad situations? What has that taught you?**

• **How does the truth of Romans 8:28 affect the way you approach life?**

Close the devotion in prayer.

PRAY **Father in heaven, we are so thankful that you are so powerful. We thank you for your love and for your care. You are amazing! You take the worst experiences of our lives and through your wisdom and power you redeem them by bringing good out of them. We praise you for this. We are so glad to serve such a mighty God. In Jesus' name, amen.**

DEVOTION 2
sugar or salt

At each table, place two small plastic cups. In one cup, put about two tablespoons of sugar; put about two tablespoons of salt in the other.

When it's time to begin the devotion, ask the women to pass the plastic cups around, examine the contents, and decide what's in them. After two or three minutes, gather the group's attention:

ASK • **Were you able to decide for certain what was in the cups?**

• **What methods did you use to determine the contents?**

SAY **At first glance, the contents of the two cups look very similar. But if you look closely, you can see that they don't look exactly the same. They don't smell quite the same either. And if you tasted them, you know that they certainly don't taste the same! The Bible talks about the need to be discerning. Listen to these verses from 1 Thessalonians. "Test everything. Hold on to the good. Avoid every kind of evil"** (1 Thessalonians 5:21-22).

With the women at your table, talk about what these verses mean. By what means do we test everything? What does the passage mean by "everything"? What is the good that we're supposed to keep and the evil we're supposed to avoid?

After a few minutes, gather the group's attention. Ask for volunteers to share their ideas.

Close the devotion in prayer.

PRAY **Father God, thank you for this experience. Thank you for teaching us that we need to be careful and discerning about everything. We know how important it is to avoid evil and to hold on to you. Sometimes, though, the things we encounter in life are so deceptive. It's hard to tell good from evil. Father, help us know the difference. And help us to do what pleases you. In Jesus' name, amen.**

DEVOTION 3
God's princesses

Set out white, silver, or yellow chenille stems (pipe cleaners) at every table. Each woman will need about ten chenille stems. If you can't find enough chenille stems, or if the cost is prohibitive, you can use aluminum foil.

As the women arrive, have them make tiaras for themselves. While they're creating, have them talk about times in their childhood when they truly felt like princesses—perhaps someone dressed up like Cinderella for Halloween, or perhaps someone had a weekly date night with her father.

Have the women wear their tiaras for the rest of the devotion.

SAY **Almost all young girls dream about being princesses. The stories we're told as children are full of princesses, from Sleeping Beauty to Cinderella. But as we grow up, we slowly realize that we will never be the princesses we dreamed of. We learn that our lives will be full of bills, cleaning, cooking, working, and errands. A life that doesn't seem nearly as much fun as balls, gowns, and jewels!**

But God's Word tells us that we're the daughters of a great king. That makes us princesses. Our lives may not seem royal, but they are. Listen to what Scripture says: "Yet to all who received him, to those who believed in his name, he gave the right to become children of God" (John 1:12).

In your small groups, discuss these questions:

• What does it mean to be a child of God?

• How does being the daughter of the King affect the way you see yourself and your role in this world?

• What rights and responsibilities go along with being a princess of God?

Give the groups a few minutes to discuss. Then have volunteers share their ideas with the rest of the group.

End the devotion with prayer.

PRAY **Father God, so often our lives feel so ordinary and boring. There are chores to do and bills to pay and errands to run. We feel run down and weary. We certainly don't feel like princesses. But we are your children, your daughters, and that is special. We know that you, the King of kings, love us. Help us to remember our position as your daughters. Help us to live our lives according to this honor. In Jesus' name, amen.**

DEVOTION 4
flower children

At each table, place bouquets of inexpensive flowers. Be sure each bouquet has an assortment of varieties and colors. And be sure to have at least one flower for each woman attending.

When you're ready to begin the devotion, have each woman choose one flower out of the bouquet that reminds her of herself. Have the women take turns around the table telling why they chose the flower they did. Perhaps she feels she's as cheery as a daisy or as vibrant as a red rose.

Next, have each woman spend two full minutes silently observing all she can about the flower she chose. Have the women chat with each other about what they've observed and answer this question: What does this flower say about the Creator?

When the women have had a chance to talk,

SAY **Our Creator is truly amazing. Not only has he created these flowers in myriad colors and varieties, but he has also created us. And we come in even more varieties than these flowers. Listen to these words from the Bible. "For you created my inmost being; you knit me together in my mother's womb. I praise you because I am fearfully and wonderfully made; your works are wonderful, I know that full well"** (Psalm 139:13-14).

Have the women discuss these questions:
- **In what ways are women as beautiful as flowers?**
- **Why did God create so many kinds of flowers?**
- **Why are there so many different kinds of women?**
- **How is the "bouquet" of women here at this church particularly lovely?**

Invite the women at each table to pray together, thanking God for creating the women at your church.

DEVOTION 5
doodles

This is a great devotion to use when your group includes some Christians and some non-Christians. Make sure that there are mature Christians who can lead the discussion at each table.

Cover each table with white paper. At each table, place several regular and colored pencils—at least one pencil per woman. Make sure there's also at least one large pencil eraser at each table.

When you're ready to begin the devotion, invite the women to take a few moments to draw doodles on the paper. After three or four minutes, call their attention. Ask the women to pass around the eraser and erase the doodles they've made.

ASK • **Was anyone able to erase her doodles so completely that you can't see the mark anymore and the paper looks completely clean?**

SAY **The Bible tells us that sin is like these doodles. All of us sin. There's not one of us who hasn't lied, cheated, or taken something, even a little something, that wasn't ours to take. Many people spend their lives feeling terrible guilt for the wrong things they've done. Other religions teach that by doing good things or by living a spiritual life you can make up for the wrong you've done. But that's not what the Bible teaches. The Bible says that there's nothing we can do to make up for our sins. It's like trying to erase pencil marks from this paper. There's no way we can make the paper look brand-new again. Listen to these words from The Living Bible. "Come, let's talk this over!" says the Lord; "no matter how deep the stain of your sins, I can take it out and make you as clean as freshly fallen snow. Even if you are stained as red as crimson, I can make you white as wool!"** (Isaiah 1:18, The Living Bible)**.**

Have the women discuss these questions at their tables:

• **How does God clean us from our sins?**

• **What do we have to do to be cleansed?**

• **Why does God do this for us?**

• **How should we respond to this news today? How should we respond for the rest of our lives?**

After a few minutes of discussion, have volunteers share their responses to the last question with the rest of the group. Then have the women break up into pairs or trios to pray, thanking God for his gift of a cleansed life.

DEVOTION 6
seasons

You'll need one item to represent each season; for example, a plastic pumpkin for fall, a winter coat for winter, a silk tulip for spring, and a swimsuit for summer. Hang one of these items on each wall of the room.

When it's time for the devotion,

SAY **I've placed items that represent the four seasons on the walls of our room. Take your chair, and move to the season that you love most. When you get there, find a partner, have a seat, and chat about why you like that season the best.**

Give the women a chance to chat. Then regain their attention.

SAY **Aren't we fortunate that our God is creative enough to provide different seasons in different parts of the world during different times of the year. Living in our world is a much richer experience because we can go to cold places and enjoy a brisk winter day or to another place and laze on a sunny beach. The Bible talks about a kind of season too. Listen to these words from the King James version:**

"To every thing there is a season, and a time to every purpose under the heaven: A time to be born, and a time to die; a time to plant, and a time to pluck up that which is planted; A time to kill, and a time to heal; a time to break down, and a time to build up; A time to weep, and a time to laugh; a time to mourn, and a time to dance; A time to cast away stones, and a time to gather stones together; a time to embrace, and a time to refrain from embracing; A time to get, and a time to lose; a time to keep, and a time to cast away; A time to rend, and a time to sew; a time to keep silence, and a time to speak; A time to love, and a time to hate; a time of war, and a time of peace" (Ecclesiastes 3:1-8).

Encourage the women to consult this passage in their own Bibles as they discuss these questions with their partner from the beginning of this devotion.

- **What is this passage talking about?**
- **Are you surprised by some of the things that the Bible says have a season or a purpose? Why or why not?**
- **What do you think is the purpose of all these seasons?**
- **What is the wisdom of this passage?**

Have the women pray together with their partners and ask God to help them understand the purpose of all the seasons of life.

DEVOTION 7
women's legacies

Cover all the tables with white paper. Place one pen per person at every table.

When it's time to start the devotion, have the women at each table brainstorm as many famous women from history as they can in five minutes. Have each table of women write down on the white paper the famous women they think of, as well as what they're famous for.

After five minutes, call time.

At each table, have the women discuss how many of the women they came up with were famous for good reasons or for bad reasons. Also, encourage them to notice how many Christian women they came up with.

Then, have the women discuss these questions:

• **What does it take to be famous?**

• **What kind of legacy did these women leave?**

• **In what ways can women affect and change the world they live in?**

Read aloud 1 Peter 2:9-12 and then discuss these questions.

• **As Christian women, how can we change the world we live in?**

• **What would you like your legacy to be?**

After a few minutes of discussion, have volunteers share their ideas with the rest of the group. Then have the women pray around the circle, asking God to help them live lives that are honoring and pleasing to him.

FIFTEEN PRAYER IDEAS

It can be difficult to lead prayer in a large group of women. Some women are experienced "pray-ers," but others are intimidated by the idea of praying in front of others. Here are some ways to facilitate prayer and to make prayer nonthreatening and fun for new Christians. These ideas will also help you break out of the rut of asking for prayer requests and then just praying aloud. You can use these ideas at banquets, retreats, Bible studies, or any other women's ministry event.

card prayers

Hand out 3x5 cards and pens. Have each woman write her name on a card and add a personal prayer request that she's comfortable sharing with someone else in the group. Then gather all the cards, shuffle them, and have each woman take one, making sure women don't get their own. Have each woman pray for the woman whose name is on the card and for the prayer request.

abc thanksgiving prayers

Have women in groups of no more than five take turns completing the sentence "Thank you, God, for…" The first woman should mention something that starts with A, the second woman something that starts with B, and so on through the alphabet.

blessing prayers

Have women get into small groups of no more than five, and hand out paper and pens to everyone. Ask each woman to write a blessing for the person on her right. Then have each woman read aloud the blessing she wrote as a prayer.

hat prayers

Put each woman's name in a hat. Have the women draw names and pray for the woman whose name they chose. If the women don't know each other well, take five to ten minutes for them to find each other, introduce themselves, and mention a prayer request. Then regain the group's attention, open in prayer, have the women pray silently for the woman whose name they chose, then close the prayer.

one-word prayers

If you have a large group, have everyone form one big circle around the perimeter of the room. Call out a topic, such as praise or request. Women should take turns around the room saying aloud one word that represents their prayer.

bubble prayers

Take the group outside. Hand out one jar of bubble solution to every four or five women. Pause for three or four minutes of silent prayer. Ask the women to quietly take turns blowing bubbles and watching them float up. Encourage the women to imagine their prayers floating up to heaven. As the bubbles float, the women should thank God for hearing their prayers.

pass the prayer

Do this prayer in groups no larger than ten. Hand out paper and pens. Ask each woman to write her name at the top of a sheet of paper. Then have the women pass the papers to their right. Ask each woman write a sentence prayer for the woman whose paper she now has. Have women pass the papers once more to the right and write a prayer for the next woman. Continue passing the prayers and writing new prayers until each woman gets her own paper. Give the women a few minutes to read the prayers the other women have written about them.

birthday-candle prayers

This is a great prayer to use on someone's birthday. You'll need a cake, matches, and enough birthday candles for everyone to have one. Give each woman a birthday candle. Have everyone think of a one-word prayer, such as "peace" or "joy," that represents what they'd like God to give the birthday person. Then, working very quickly, light the first birthday candle, put it in the cake, and say the one-word prayer. Have the next woman light her candle from the first one, put it in the cake, and say her one-word prayer. Continue quickly until all the candles are lit. Have the birthday woman blow out the candles, and have everyone call out "amen!"

candy prayers

Place a big bowl of assorted candies on each table. For example, you might want to use an assortment of lemon drops, peppermints, chocolate kisses, and Starburst candies. Have everyone pray a prayer of thanksgiving for the person on her right by choosing a candy out of the bowl that somehow describes the person they're praying for. For example, a person might pray, "Thank you, God, for my friends' cheerfulness. She's as bright and cheery as this lemon drop."

prayer sisters

Pair up women with women they don't know very well. Have the women become prayer sisters for a month. Have them commit to pray for each other at least four times a week. Have the pairs communicate by phone, at church, or by e-mail to connect and share their prayer requests with each other.

smile prayers

This prayer works great when your group is really large. Have the women form a large circle around the perimeter of the room and hold hands. Invite the women to glance around the room, noticing one another, and silently praying for individual women they see.

Have the women smile at whoever they are praying for as they pray. After three or four minutes, close the prayer.

e-mail prayers

Ask each woman to give her e-mail address to the woman on her right. Encourage each woman to go home and type a prayer for the woman whose e-mail address she has and send the prayer to her.

lipstick prayers

You'll need several mirror tiles and several old lipsticks. You'll need at least one mirror tile and one lipstick for every five women. Place the tiles and lipsticks on tables. When it's time for prayer, invite the women to go to the prayer table, pray a brief prayer of praise, and then use the lipstick to draw a word or a symbol that represents what they prayed about.

rock prayers

You'll need at least four or five small stones per woman. You'll also need one clean, tall plastic waste can (filled with water) for every ten women.

Pile the stones at the back of the room on a table. Place the waste cans at the front of the room. Wait until you've placed them at the front before you fill them with water—they'll be very heavy.

When it's time to pray, invite the women to think of the sins that have plagued them. Invite them to go silently to the stone pile and pick up stones that will represent sins that burden them and weigh them down. Then have the women slowly carry the stones to the front of the room as they talk to God about laying aside their burdensome sins. When they get to the front of the room, have them drop the stones one by one into the water as they confess their sins to God. As they watch the stones sink to the bottom, have them thank God for burying their sins and taking away their burden.

This entire prayer activity should be done in silence and with reverence. You may want to play quiet instrumental music.

thank and ask prayers

This prayer activity makes prayer easy for women who are new to it. Have each woman think of one thing that she'd like to thank God for and one thing she'd like to ask God for; for example, a woman might want to thank God for salvation and ask God for help in a job search. Go around the room, and invite each woman to pray aloud, saying, "I thank God for…I ask God for…"

This prayer can be adapted so that the women pray for a friend rather than for themselves.✿

section **four**

Bible
STUDIES

Bible studies are the core of every women's ministry.
In this section are ten stand-alone Bible studies that can be used at any women's ministry event.

These studies will work well whether your group includes ten or fewer women or more than a hundred women. Plan to have the women sit around tables with five to ten women at each table. Photocopy the Bible studies, and give one copy to each participant.

The Bible studies are written to the participants. The activities are all developed to be self-directed. There are times in each study, however, when the group leader is called upon. Be sure to read the study and be prepared to lead the group from the front when necessary. Also be sure to gather all the supplies requested.

Plan for these Bible studies to last anywhere from forty-five minutes to an hour and fifteen minutes. Some groups, especially groups of women who don't know one another well, will answer questions very quickly. Other groups will spend more time on the discussion because they are more comfortable with others in the group or just because they like to talk more. If you have a large group of fifty or more women, the studies will take longer because it will take longer for all the table groups to report what they've discussed to the entire group when that is called for.

Feel free to adapt these studies to your group's needs. Add or delete questions or Scripture passages. Change the supplies or the prayer activity. You may want to use some of the prayer ideas on page 79 if you are working with women who are not used to praying aloud.

Most important, enjoy these Bible studies, and use them to help the women in your group grow closer to God and understand their relationship with him better.

STUDY 1

Wisdom

Abigail (1 Samuel 25:2-42)

The Opener

> Leader: You'll need to provide a basket and a pen and three 2x8½-inch paper slips for each woman.

Begin today's Bible study by writing three "proverbs for wise women" on the slips of paper your leader gives you. For inspiration, think about what wise women think, do, and say.

When everyone has finished, the leader will collect all the proverbs in a basket. Take three proverbs from the basket as it's passed around, making sure you don't get your own. Read the proverbs aloud. Then discuss these questions together:

• How were these proverbs similar or different from each other?
• What does it mean to be a wise woman?
• Do women value wisdom?

The Bible Study

Have someone read aloud the story of Abigail from 1 Samuel 25.

✿ What character qualities did Abigail possess that made her such an incredible woman?

✿ Abigail's wisdom is revealed not only in what she did, but also in her timing. Where do we see this? Why is doing the right thing at the right time an indication of wisdom?

✿ In what ways did Abigail understand people, love people, and help people? Do you think these traits are characteristic of a wise person? Explain.

✿ What else does this story say about wisdom—what wisdom is, how to use it, and where to get it?

✿ What happens when Christians act with the foolishness of Nabal or the wisdom of Abigail?

✿ Do you feel that Christians are generally wise people? Why or why not?

✿ Why is true wisdom so rare among people? Do you think we discourage the pursuit of wisdom in young Christians? Why or why not?

✿ What could we do to make wisdom a more sought-after trait among Christians? How can we teach our daughters to be wise like Abigail?

✿ How do we ourselves pursue wisdom? What do you think your life would be like if you were wiser?

The Closing

Find two other women to talk to. Take turns sharing with one another the situations in your life in which you need more wisdom than you currently have. Take a few minutes to pray for one another, asking God to give you and your friends wisdom.

> Leader: Close the Bible study time with prayer. Be sure to take time to ask the women for individual prayer requests. Have women write these requests below and continue to pray for one another later.

Prayer Requests

STUDY 2
Beauty
1 Peter 3:3-4

The Opener

> Leader: You'll need to bring in several fashion magazines for this activity.

Form groups of two or three, and take turns talking about the most beautiful woman you've ever known. Tell your partners why you thought the woman was beautiful.

Next, look at one of the fashion magazines your leader will pass around. Talk about which women are considered to be beautiful in our society. Do they share the same characteristics as the women you find beautiful?

After a few minutes, your leader will gather the entire group's attention. Discuss these questions:

• What does it mean to be beautiful in the eyes of the world?
• Is it right for Christian women to want to be beautiful? Why or why not?

The Bible Study

✿ How has the issue of beauty affected your own life? When have you felt beautiful? When have you felt that you weren't beautiful? Share at least one story with the others in your group.

Read 1 Corinthians 6:19-20.
✿ What, if anything, do you think this passage has to do with beauty?

Read 1 Peter 3:3-4.
✿ What does it mean to be beautiful? Why is inner beauty important?

✿ Is outer beauty unimportant? When can the pursuit of outer beauty get us into trouble?

✿ How does the Bible's definition of beauty clash with society's definition of beauty? What makes it difficult to be a Christian woman in today's world?

✿ As Christian women who live in this world, how are we to reconcile the differences between what society demands and what the Bible calls us to?

✿ In at least one way, the Bible and the women's liberation movement have something in common: They both say women should be valued for something beyond appearance. In what ways, though, does the Bible call women to a better understanding of beautiful womanhood?

✿ As Christian women, we can struggle with issues of appearance and beauty. Through the years, different Christian groups have come to different conclusions about what is appropriate for women in terms of dress and appearance. Discuss how Christian women can decide how to handle the following issues in light of what the Bible says about beauty.

• Wearing makeup

• Cosmetic surgery

• Diet and weight loss

• Exercise

• Hair color

• Jewelry

• Piercings

• Clothing

✿ If you were teaching a group of young women about what it means to be truly beautiful, what would you say?

✿ Is the advice you'd give to young women advice you need to follow yourself? How do you need to change your attitude about being beautiful?

The Closing

Find one or two other women to talk to. Together, come up with a list of "beauty treatments" that will help you develop the kind of beauty God wants you to have. Tell each other the treatments you will take to become more beautiful.

In a few minutes, your leader will call for your attention. Be ready to share your list of beauty treatments with the rest of the group.

> Leader: Close the Bible study time with prayer. Be sure to take time to ask the women for individual prayer requests. Have women write these requests below and continue to pray for one another later.

Prayer Requests

STUDY 3

Purpose and Calling

Esther

The Opener

Form small groups of two or three. Choose at least three women from the list below, and talk about what you think each of the women you chose feels (or felt) her purpose or calling is (or was).

Mother Teresa	Corrie ten Boom
Hillary Rodham Clinton	Ellen DeGeneres
Danielle Steel	Katie Couric
Alice Walker	Amelia Earhart
Lucille Ball	Princess Diana
Rachel Carson	Harriet Tubman

In a few minutes, your group leader will have you gather in one large group. Share the ideas your small group had with the entire group. Then discuss these questions with the large group:
• How important is it to have a sense of purpose or calling in life?
• Do you feel women today generally have a strong sense of calling? Explain.
• What role does purpose have in the Christian woman's life?

The Bible Study

> Leader: The story of Esther is too long to read it all during one Bible study session. Be sure to read the story and be familiar with it enough to summarize the story before you begin this Bible study.

Read Esther 2:5-18.
✿ How did it happen that Esther became queen? How do you see God's hand in what happened to her?

✿ Do you think Esther was prepared to be queen? How does God prepare people for what he plans for them to do?

Read Esther 2:19-20; 4:1-17.
✿ What risks did Esther take? Why do you think she was willing to take these risks? Think about your own life—does following God's plans always involve taking risks?

Reread Esther 4:14-17.
✿ What do you think made Esther decide to go through with the plan to talk to the king about Haman's evil scheme?

✿ Mordecai told Esther that this opportunity might be the reason she's been put in this position. Have you ever felt that God had put you in a specific time and place to accomplish a certain thing? Tell the group about your experience.

✿ How did you (or do you) know what God had planned for you to do?

✿ Do you think Esther was scared about approaching the king? Worried? Excited? Determined? How do you think we should feel about God's purpose for our lives?

Form two groups. In one group, read Esther 7:1-10. In the other group, read Esther 8:1-16. Form one group again, and talk about these questions.
✿ Esther was successful in bringing Haman's evil scheme to light. Do you think that we will always be successful? What does it mean to be successful?

✿ How can you find God's purpose for your life and do it? What concerns you about this? What excites you?

The Closing

> Leader: If possible, play the Wayne Watson song "For Such a Time As This" before moving on with the closing activity. Also, be sure to have paper and pens available for the closing activity.

On a sheet of paper, write, "For such a time as this…" Then take five minutes to reflect silently on your life. Consider the unique situation of your life, and think about your unique concerns, passions, and abilities. For what purpose do you think God has called you? Write as many ideas as you can in the five minutes you've been given. Then, when your leader directs you to, find a partner to share your ideas with. Pray together with your partner, and ask God to guide you both. Make a promise to continue praying for your partner about her purpose in life.

> Leader: Close the Bible study time with prayer. Be sure to take time to ask the women for individual prayer requests. Have women write these requests below and continue to pray for one another later.

Prayer Requests

STUDY 4
Contentment
Philippians 4:11-13

The Opener

Form pairs or trios. Then find something on your person that brings you a sense of contentment. For example, maybe you're wearing a piece of jewelry that was given to you by someone you love deeply, or maybe you're carrying a quotation in your wallet that inspires you. Share thoughts about the item you found with your partner or with the others in your trio.

Next, find something in your pocket or purse, or even in the room, that symbolizes a way that women look for contentment inappropriately. For example, a dollar bill might symbolize looking for contentment in wealth. Share the items you've found with the others in your small group.

After you've talked, your leader will call the entire group back together. Discuss these questions together:

• What is contentment?

• Why do we long for contentment, and why is it so elusive?

• What misunderstandings do you think women have about contentment?

The Bible Study

✿ When have you experienced true contentment?

Read Hebrews 13:5.

✿ Why is it so hard to be content with what we have? Do you think being content is harder or easier in today's society than it was when this Scripture was written?

Read 1 Timothy 6:6-10.

✿ Why is it dangerous to be discontented? What have you observed about people who are discontented?

✿ What kinds of healthy or unhealthy things do people do to overcome their discontentment? Do these things work?

✿ Women in particular seem to struggle with being discontented. Why can this be such a problem for women? How has discontentment affected your own life?

✿ Is it ever good to be discontented? Why or why not?

Read Matthew 7:11 and James 1:17.
✿ What does our discontentment say about our relationship with God or our understanding of God? Do you think we can remain discontented if we nurture our connection with God? Explain.

Read Proverbs 19:23.
✿ Does this proverb ring true for you, or does it seem too simplistic? Explain. How can the fear of the Lord lead to contentment? How do we cultivate that in our lives and find true satisfaction?

Read Philippians 4:11-13.

✿ Do you think it's really possible to be content in all circumstances? Have you ever known anyone who was truly content? Explain.

✿ Is there such a thing as contentment apart from God? Explain.

The Closing

Find a partner, and play the "If only" game. Take turns completing the statement, "If only I had…; then…" or "If only I were…; then…" with things that lead women to be discontented. For example, someone might say, "If only I had the perfect hairstyle, then my whole life would come together." After one partner completes an "If only" statement, the other partner should respond, "But godliness with contentment is great gain." Continue until each partner has had a chance to complete several "If only" statements.

Then tell your partner about a situation in your life where you struggle to be content. Pray for your partner, and ask God to help her find his peace and contentment. Be sure to show your partner great respect and love by keeping your discussion private between the two of you.

> Leader: Close the Bible study time with prayer. Be sure to take time to ask the women for individual prayer requests. Have women write these requests below and continue to pray for one another later.

Prayer Requests

STUDY 5
Confidence
Jeremiah 17:5-8 and 1 Peter 1:3-9

The Opener

To begin today's Bible study, remember what you were like as a young teenager (thirteen to fourteen years old). Think specifically about how self-confident you were. Mark your level of self-confidence on the line below, with 1 meaning you were completely lacking in confidence and 10 meaning you were ready to take on the world! Then find at least one person to chat with. Show her what rating you gave yourself, and explain what life was like for you as a young teenager.

1	2	3	4	5	6	7	8	9	10

After a few minutes, your group leader will gather the entire group. Discuss these questions:
- Why do young girls struggle so much with self-confidence?
- Do you feel that a lack of self-confidence is something girls generally outgrow, or does it continue to plague us as women?
- What do women or girls do to overcome a lack of self-confidence?

The Bible Study

Read Jeremiah 17:5-6.

✿ What have you noticed about women who trust in themselves? What happens when women trust in themselves?

✿ When is being self-confident bad? When is it good?

✿ Some women have a tendency to be too humble. What does the Bible mean when it differentiates between trusting in self and trusting in God?

✿ Tell about a time you trusted in yourself inappropriately. What happened, and how did your experience affect your understanding of yourself and God?

Read Jeremiah 17:7-8.
✿ How is the person whose confidence is in the Lord different? How is her experience of life different?

✿ Take note of the promises in Jeremiah 17:7-8. What evidence of these promises do you see in your life and in the lives of other Christians as you all put your confidence in God?

✿ Tell about a time you put your trust in God. What made this experience different from the time you trusted in yourself?

✿ What is the right attitude to have about self?

Read 1 Peter 1:3-9.
✿ This passage speaks of the confidence and hope we have in Jesus Christ. Why can we be confident in God? How have you experienced this?

✿ What difference would putting your confidence in God every day make in your life?

✿ What's holding you back? What do you need to do to overcome those obstacles?

The Closing

Find two or three other women to talk with. Take turns completing this sentence, "When I put my confidence in myself…"

When everyone's had a chance to complete that sentence, take turns completing this sentence, "When I put my confidence in God…"

Tell each other what you plan to do to put your confidence in God today. Pray for each other, asking God to help each of you follow through on your plans to put your confidence in him.

> Leader: Close the Bible study time with prayer. Be sure to take time to ask the women for individual prayer requests. Have women write these requests below and continue to pray for one another later.

Prayer Requests

STUDY 6
Encouragement
Mary and Elizabeth (Luke 1:5-80)

The Opener

> Leader: You'll need to bring in an assortment of note cards and envelopes,
> as well as stamps. You'll need at least one card for each woman attending the study.
> You may also want to bring in a church directory and a local phone book so
> women can address the cards they've written.

To begin today's Bible study, take a note card from your leader, and write a short note to a friend who could use a little encouragement.

After everyone's had a chance to finish her note, your leader will gather the group's attention. Together with the entire group, discuss these questions:
- What's the most encouraging thing someone has ever said to you?
- Why is encouragement so important?
- What would our lives be like if no one ever encouraged us?

The Bible Study
Read Luke 1:26-38.
✿ How do you suppose Mary, a young, unwed peasant girl, felt at this point? Why did she need encouragement? Have you ever needed encouragement as much as Mary did? Tell the group about your experience.

Read Luke 1:39-45.

✿ What do we know about Elizabeth? (You may want to look at Luke 1:5-24 to review Elizabeth's story.)

✿ Elizabeth immediately had a word of encouragement for Mary. How do you think she knew what to say? How do you suppose Mary responded to this encouragement?

✿ How were Elizabeth's words a confirmation and a comfort for Mary?

✿ How has the encouragement of others affected your life? In contrast, how has the discouragement of others affected your life?

Read 1 Thessalonians 5:11.

✿ What does it take to be a good encourager? Do you think women are natural encouragers? Explain.

✿ Do you think that in today's society women are less likely to encourage each other than in Mary and Elizabeth's time? Why or why not?

✿ What keeps women from being encouraging? How can we overcome all of those obstacles so that we can support each other the way God wants us to?

✿ Why is encouragement so powerful? After all, encouragement is only words.

✿ What will you need to do today, tomorrow, and next week to become an encourager?

The Closing

Spend the next five minutes spreading encouragement through your group. At your leader's invitation, stand up and mingle, encouraging each woman you see. Keep encouraging others until your leader calls time. Then return to your seat.

After the Bible study is over, don't forget to mail the cards you wrote at the beginning of the meeting.

> Leader: Close the Bible study time with prayer. Be sure to take time to ask the women for individual prayer requests. Have women write these requests below and continue to pray for one another later.

Prayer Requests

STUDY 7
Hope

The Opener

Find a partner, and tell her about these two things: something you hope for, and something that gives you hope.

After a few minutes, your leader will call for your attention. Be ready to share your ideas with the rest of the group. Then with the entire group, discuss these questions:

- What is hope?
- Why is hope so important to people? What is it like to be hopeless?
- Where does hope come from?

The Bible Study

✿ What makes our world sometimes seem like a hopeless place to live?

✿ Tell about a time you hoped for something but were disappointed. What kinds of thoughts, emotions, and actions does this kind of disappointment cause?

✿ Where do people look for hope? Why are people so often disappointed in their hopes?

✿ What hopeful messages do you find in Isaiah 40:25-31? Why is hoping in God different than another kind of hope?

✿ Though we know that God is good and trustworthy, we still sometimes find ourselves disappointed in God. Tell about a time you were disappointed with God.

✿ When we are disappointed with God, does the fault lie with God or with us? Explain.

Read Psalm 37:3-7 and Romans 8:28.
✿ What can we do when we feel disappointed with God?

Read Romans 5:1-5 and 12:12.
✿ Why is it hard to hope in distressing times? How does this counsel from the Bible help you develop your own hope in God?

✿ Tell about a time you did put your hope in God despite your circumstances. What happened? What lessons did you learn about God?

✿ What would your life be like if you hoped 100 percent in God's goodness, his wisdom, his timing, and his plans for you?

✿ How can we find joy in hoping in God? How can you increase your hope in God today?

The Closing

Find two or three women to talk with.

The Bible says that having hope is like soaring with the eagles. Come up with your own analogies about what having hope is like. Then talk about how you put your hope in God when you're facing a tough situation.

When your leader calls for your attention, be ready to share your ideas with the rest of the group.

> Leader: Close the Bible study time with prayer. Be sure to take time to ask the women for individual prayer requests. Have women write these requests below and continue to pray for one another later.

Prayer Requests

STUDY 8

The 1 Thing

Mary and Martha (Luke 10:38-42)

The Opener

> Leader: You'll need to provide paper and scissors for all the women.

Take a minute or two to jot down the priorities you've made for your life. Then number the items according to what's most import, second-most important, and so on.

Next, find a partner, and compare your lists. With your partner, discuss these questions.

- How did you come by the priorities you wrote down? How do people set our priorities in life?
- Does the way you live your life reflect your priorities? Why or why not?

The Bible Study

Read Luke 10:38-42.

✿ Why do you think Jesus went to Mary and Martha's home?

✿ How would you describe Mary's and Martha's relationships with Jesus?

✿ Both Mary and Martha loved Jesus and wanted to serve him. Why do you think Martha's service was not received in the same way that Mary's was?

✿ Did Jesus love Mary more than he loved Martha? How do you know that? Did Mary love Jesus more than Martha? How do you know that?

✿ What is Jesus really saying here? Why was Martha's busyness inappropriate? How are we to do what Jesus says and still get done all the things that need to be taken care of?

✿ Do you think Martha's problem is a uniquely feminine problem? Why is it so easy to let responsibilities and chores get in the way of our relationship with Christ?

✿ When do you experience the Martha syndrome? How has an inappropriate attention to work affected your life? What have you done to overcome it?

✿ Have you ever experienced a time you did put your relationship with Jesus first? What happened, and how did it affect your life?

✿ What will it take for you to start sitting at Jesus' feet and listening to what he has to say?

✿ How will your life change when you do this?

The Closing

> Leader: Hand out paper and scissors to the women.

Find one or two other women to talk to.

Take a sheet of paper and a pair of scissors, and cut a large numeral 1 from the paper. Talk about the one thing that Jesus said was important. How can you make that one thing your priority in life? Jot down your ideas on your cutout 1 as you talk.

Pray for each other, asking God to help you keep your priorities straight.

After the meeting is over, take your notes home and put them in a place that will remind you to keep first things first.

> Leader: Close the Bible study time with prayer. Be sure to take time to ask the women for individual prayer requests. Have women write these requests below and continue to pray for one another later.

Prayer Requests

STUDY 9
Friendship
Ruth and Naomi (Ruth 1–4)

The Opener

Find two other women to chat with. Take turns talking about one of these two topics:

- How did you get along with your sisters when you were growing up? What are your favorite memories of being a sister?
- Who did you hang out with in high school or college? What are your fondest memories about your group of friends?

After you've chatted for a few minutes, your group leader will call for your attention. Together, you'll discuss these questions:

- Why is friendship so important?
- What does it take to be a friend as an adult woman in our culture?

The Bible Study

> Leader: The story of Ruth and Naomi is too long to read it all during one Bible study session. Be sure to read the story and be familiar with it so that you can summarize the story before you begin this Bible study.

Read Ruth 1.

✿ God brought two women from entirely different worlds together. What were their similarities? What were their differences? When have you had a friendship with someone very different from you?

❀ What did Ruth's commitment to Naomi, despite the death of her husband, reveal about her character? Has someone ever been that devoted to you? What happened? What did that friendship mean to you?

❀ Do you think women have this kind of devoted friendships today? Why or why not?

❀ What gets in the way of such committed relationships?

Read Ruth 2:1-7.
❀ What do you admire most about the relationship between Ruth and Naomi?

Read Ruth 3:1-4.

✿ What can you learn about friendship through the relationship between Ruth and Naomi?

✿ Do you think the way Christians approach friendships with one another today pleases God? Why or why not?

✿ What do you think God intends for us (or expects from us) in our relationships with one another? How are we going to do that today?

✿ What do you have to gain from developing intimate friendships with other women? How would these friendships benefit your church? your community? the world?

✿ What habits or attitudes must be overcome so that we can really become better friends with one another?

The Closing

Find someone in the room you don't know very well. Take a few minutes to talk about today's Bible study. What lessons did you learn about being a friend?

Next, take just five minutes to get to know each other better. If you can, make plans to share a cup of coffee, share a phone call, or take a walk together later this week to develop your new friendship. Be sure to follow through with your plans!

> Leader: Close the Bible study time with prayer. Be sure to take time to ask the women for individual prayer requests. Have women write these requests below and continue to pray for one another later.

Prayer Requests

STUDY 10

Significance

The Woman of Noble Character (Proverbs 31:10-31)

Leader: Please provide ten paper plates and a marker for each woman.

The Opener

Begin your time together with prayer. Then warmly welcome the women.

Think about all the things you're responsible for in your day-to-day life. Write those thing on the paper plates your leader will give you, one per plate.

When everyone's finished, get into trios to share what you've written on your plates with one another. Then discuss these questions in your trio:

- What does it mean to be a woman in the twenty-first century?
- How do you keep all of your "plates" in the air? Do the responsibilities in your life make you feel empowered or just tired? Explain.
- What in your life makes you feel significant and valued?

The Bible Study

✿ What challenges do women face today as they look for their role in society?

✿ How do we find significance in our roles as women today?

✿ What challenges our feelings of value and significance?

Have someone read aloud Proverbs 31:10-31 while everyone else follows along in their Bibles.
✿ What someone does reflects who she is. What does this passage tell us about who this woman is?

✿ What do you think gave this woman a sense of significance and belonging?

✿ How do we know that her worth was based on more than accomplishments? What was the true source of her significance?

✿ What does it mean to be virtuous? Why does God value virtuous women?

✿ What do you most admire about this woman? In what ways is she an example to you?

✿ Do you think being a woman is more or less special than in previous generations? Explain.

✿ What about this woman's example do you find challenging? Do you think God wants us to follow her example completely? Explain.

❀ Which of this woman's characteristics would you like to incorporate into your own life? How can you begin doing that?

The Closing

Proverbs 31:10-31 says that a woman of noble character is worth far more than rubies. Take five minutes to talk with the trio you began this Bible study with. Here's your assignment:

- Update this passage for the twenty-first century. Talk about what it means to be a woman of noble character in today's world.
- Discuss why it's so important today for women of God to be of noble character.

When your leader calls for your attention, be ready to share your trio's insights with the entire group.

> Leader: Close the Bible study time with prayer. Be sure to take time to ask the women for individual prayer requests. Have women write these requests below and continue to pray for one another later.

Prayer Requests

girls movie
NIGHTS

Having a regular Girls Movie Night is bound to be a hit in your group. We live in a very media-savvy world, and it often happens that movies can express issues and truths (or even lies) in a more compelling way than a Bible study or a talk can. Here are some hints to make Girls' Movie Night a success in your group.

Hold these events on a regular basis. Once a month or once a quarter would work well. If at all possible, have women get together in one another's homes. This will make their time together more intimate and comfortable, and the women will feel much more comfortable sharing after the movie if they feel at home.

Make sure that someone in the group reviews the movie to check that it's appropriate for the group. Not everyone will enjoy every movie. On the other hand, everyone should be willing to give the chosen movie a try. The important part of the event is not just enjoying the movie, but being able to draw spiritual lessons from the film. You may want to have the hostess choose the movie.

Serve food! An easy arrangement is to have the hostess provide the munchies. If the group meets in a different home each time, a different person will be responsible for food each time. Some women may want to serve elaborate, fancy cakes or cookies. Others might just have a bag of chips and some store-bought dip. Others may order pizza or whip up a three-course meal. Some women may want to tie the refreshments to the setting or theme of the movie. Anything goes! Just be sure to have fun and to encourage the women not to try to one-up each other with the refreshments.

Keep it casual and friendly. This isn't a dress-up affair. People should be encouraged to take off their shoes, sit on the floor, and make themselves comfortable. Girls Movie Night is a time to get to know one another and make friends.

Keep the groups small, probably no more than ten women. Some of the discussions after the movie can get intense and personal. It's hard to bare your soul to fifty women. In a small group, each person will have more chances to talk. Smaller groups will encourage depth and intimacy, and people will be better able to form really deep friendships. If lots of women are interested in movie nights, organize several groups.

Arrange for child care somewhere else. The women who come need to be able to enjoy the movie and the discussion without worrying about their children and without being distracted by another woman's clinging or crying child. Plus, there are some topics that just can't be discussed in front of children.

Keep the discussions casual. This get-together isn't a Bible study or a film class. The questions listed with each movie are provided to prompt people to explore the spiritual issues raised in the movie and to talk about their own lives and their own relationships with God. Be sensitive to those who are deeply moved by a film. For some, a movie might bring up painful memories—they may need to talk about those memories, or they may not feel like talking at all. Don't worry if some people don't get as much out of a movie as others do. Not everyone will connect with or "get" every movie.

Be sensitive to people's time. It's tough to leave a really good discussion, but some women will need to go home to children and families. Consider calling an end to the discussion after an hour or

an hour and a half so that women who need to can make a grace-
ful exit without feeling guilty. On the other hand, in some groups,
talking until the wee hours might be completely appropriate.
Know what's appropriate for your group.

Last, be sure to enjoy this time together, relaxing with friends
and sisters in Christ!

MOVIE 1
Chocolat (2000)
Genre: Drama/Romance
Length: About 120 minutes
Rating: PG-13

Plot: Vianne, a single mother in the late 1950s, moves into a small French village and opens a chocolate shop during Lent. Most in the town instantly dislike or mistrust her, though they are enchanted by the wonderful chocolate delicacies she creates.

Discussion Starter Questions:

❀ What does this movie have to say about legalism and self-righteousness versus freedom?

❀ Why is judging others so dangerous?

❀ What does this movie have to say about welcoming and accepting people?

❀ What lessons can be learned about friendship and helping others?

❀ Based on this movie, what would you say are the basic needs of people? How are those needs met?

MOVIE 2
Joe Versus the Volcano (1990)

Genre: Allegorical fantasy

Length: About 100 minutes

Rating: PG

Plot: Joe, a downtrodden copywriter and hypochondriac, is diagnosed with a terminal "brain cloud." Since Joe hasn't long to live, a businessman hires Joe to throw himself into a volcano on a small South Pacific island to appease the gods the islanders believe in, thus securing a business deal. Joe's adventure changes his life.

Discussion Starter Questions:

✿ In the beginning of the movie, what's Joe's life like? What's got him down?

✿ How is Joe's life like the lives of most people we know? How is it different?

✿ How does Joe's adventure change him?

✿ In the movie, Patricia Graynamore says, "My father says almost the whole world's asleep. Everybody you know, everybody you see, everybody you talk to. He says only a few people are awake. And they live in a state of constant, total amazement." In what ways are Christians "awake"? Why can Christians live in a state of constant, total amazement?

✿ Do you need to wake up? Why or why not?

✿ How do you think God is calling you to live your life?

MOVIE 3
Enchanted April (1992)
Genre: Drama
Length: About 95 minutes
Rating: PG

Plot: Four women seeking rest and renewal come to Italy for a month. While there, they discover themselves and become fast friends.

Discussion Starter Questions:

✿ All four of the women in this movie were heartsick and weary. What had caused each woman to feel this way?

✿ How did the time in Italy revive the women?

✿ How are women today heartsick and weary?

✿ Do women today have avenues for restorative rest like this? How can women today renew their spirits?

✿ Describe how the women's friendships developed over the course of the movie. Why are friendships among women so important?

✿ How can we become better friends with other women?

✿ What other spiritual lessons did you learn from this movie?

MOVIE 4
Hope Floats (1998)
Genre: Drama/Romance
Length: About 115 minutes
Rating: PG-13

Plot: Birdee is a guest on a national talk show expecting a makeover when, instead, her best friend reveals she's having an affair with Birdee's husband. Heartbroken, she leaves the marriage to move in with her mother. Birdee struggles to put her life back together, while caring for her young daughter and deciding what to do about Justin, an old high school friend looking for romance.

Discussion Starter Questions:

✿ When Birdee left Smithville, it appeared that she had everything going for her. When she came back, her life was in ruins. What does this say about the unpredictable nature of life?

✿ How did Birdee react to her trials? How is that similar or different from the way you react to trials?

✿ What challenges did Birdee face as she tried to get her life back together again?

✿ Why was Birdee's daughter Bernice so angry with her mother? How did she become disillusioned with her father?

✿ How does Bernice's heartbreak show the vulnerability of children?

✿ How did Birdee's family serve as both an irritation and a source of strength? How is that similar to families in real life?

✿ In what sense does hope float in the movie?

✿ Where does our hope come from? Do you think hope floats in our lives?

MOVIE 5
Babette's Feast (1987)

Genre: Drama

Length: About 100 minutes

Rating: G

Danish with English subtitles

Plot: A refugee from Paris moves in with two religious sisters who live in a small village in Denmark. When she wins the lottery, she fixes a sumptuous meal to celebrate the one-hundredth birthday of the sisters' father.

Discussion Starter Questions:

✿ Describe the spiritual life of the people in this village? What was good about it? What was bad about it?

✿ In what ways do Christians today fall into the same traps?

✿ Is the kind of sacrifice the sisters made virtuous? Why or why not?

✿ What is remarkable about Babette's life and character?

✿ How is this movie a metaphor for the abundant life that God promises us?

✿ What can you do to enjoy the opulent abundance of God more fully?

MOVIE 6
The Remains of the Day (1993)
Genre: Drama
Length: About 135 minutes
Rating: PG

Plot: Stevens has spent his career as the devoted and disciplined butler of a large English estate during the middle of the twentieth century. When the new owner of the estate insists that Stevens take a vacation, Stevens reflects on his career (which the audience sees in flashbacks) during a drive across England to visit an old friend and realizes that his devotion has been misguided.

Discussion Starter Questions:

✿ What makes this movie so sad and heartbreaking?

✿ How did Stevens's devotion to duty prove to be his fatal flaw? In what ways can we be so devoted to our duty that we completely miss what we should be doing?

✿ In what ways are duty and emotion at war in this movie? Do you see a similar struggle between doing and feeling in real life?

✿ How did Stevens justify his wasted and misguided life?

✿ What does the title *The Remains of the Day* mean?

✿ What small hope are we left with at the end of the movie?

✿ As you consider your own life, looking back on past successes and failures and looking forward to your future, what spiritual lessons can you apply from this movie?

MOVIE 7
Pleasantville (1998)
Genre: Comedy
Length: About 125 minutes
Rating: PG-13

Plot: Two modern-day teenagers are transported through the television to live in a black-and-white 1950s sitcom. It's an innocent and naive place, but it's also shallow and narrow-minded. As the teenagers introduce new ideas to the television characters, people begin turning from black and white into color.

Discussion Starter Questions:

✿ In what ways did the residents of Pleasantville lead narrow lives?

✿ What caused them to change into color?

✿ Why was this so frightening for some? Why did it lead to prejudice and mistrust in some of the town residents?

✿ What lessons does this movie have for those who live in fear or prejudice?

✿ In what ways are we like the black-and-white residents of Pleasantville before we know Christ? How does life with Jesus bring color to our lives?

MOVIE 8
The Color Purple (1985)

Genre: Drama

Length: About 155 minutes

Rating: PG-13 (Some women may be offended by a
homosexual story line that's a part of this movie.)

Plot: Celie is a sharecropper's daughter living in rural Georgia in the early 1900s. She's unattractive, unloved, and a victim of incest. Her only option is to marry an unfaithful man who abuses her and eventually brings his mistress into the house. The movie follows Celie throughout her life as she searches for, and eventually finds, love and God and as she triumphs over her circumstances.

Discussion Starter Questions:

✿ What in this story moves you the most?

✿ Which character in this story do you relate to the most? the least? Why?

✿ How do our hurts and struggles affect the way we understand and relate to God?

✿ How does the color purple help Celie believe in God? What makes God real to you?

✿ What misconceptions about God do the characters in this movie have?

✿ What lessons about God's faithfulness and love do you see in this movie?

MOVIE 9

Places in the Heart (1984)

Genre: Drama

Length: About 110 minutes

Rating: PG

Plot: Edna's sheriff husband is accidentally killed by a young black boy during the Depression. To make ends meet, she takes in a blind boarder, who earns his way by making brooms, and a black man, who helps her raise a crop of cotton. Through tragedy and hardship, the characters learn to help each other, survive tough times, and extend grace.

Discussion Starter Questions:

✿ Edna, Moze and Mr. Will each took risks to help one another and, as a result, became a supportive community. What similar relationships do you have in your own life? How is true community formed?

✿ How did each character in this story respond to adversity? How does God want us to respond to the hard times we face?

✿ What roles do forgiveness and acceptance play throughout this story?

✿ Who was present in the church service taking communion? How is this a poignant and beautiful picture of God's grace?

MOVIE 10
Groundhog Day (1993)
Genre: Comedy/Fantasy/Romance

Length: About 100 minutes

Rating: PG

Plot: An abrasive weatherman named Phil discovers he's repeating the same February 2nd over...and over...and over. Unfortunately for Phil, he's the only one who knows what's happening. He decides to—mostly by trial and error—turn February 2nd into a perfect day.

Discussion Starter Questions
✿ If you could build a perfect day for yourself, what would it be like? What and who would be in it?

✿ If you could relive any one day of your life and try to improve it, what day would you choose? What would you do differently?

✿ Phil was enough of a jerk that few people liked him. He learned to change his personality, or at least hide enough of it that his colleague changed her mind about him. Do you think people can change fundamentally? Why or why not?

MOVIE 11
The Spitfire Grill (1996)
Genre: Drama
Length: About 115 minutes
Rating: PG-13

Plot: Percy, a young woman just released from prison, moves to a small town in Maine and becomes a waitress at a small restaurant. The owner of the restaurant is an older woman who decides to hold a contest to sell the restaurant. Everyone has secrets from his or her past, and healing comes to the town's residents as the secrets become known.

Discussion Starter Questions:

✿ How did suspicion affect the characters in this movie?

✿ How has suspicion, mistrust, or stereotyping affected your life?

✿ Percy suffered bad breaks her whole life. How did that affect her? How did she rise above her circumstances?

✿ Did the confession at the end of the movie surprise you? How do you think Nahum's confession affected him, his family, and the town? Why is confession so powerful?

✿ What was different about the attitude of the townspeople at the beginning of the movie and their attitude at the end of the movie? What brought about that change? How does God bring about that kind of change in us?

MOVIE 12
Persuasion (1995)
Genre: Romance
Length: About 105 minutes
Rating: PG

Plot: Anne Elliott is an unmarried woman in England during the early 1800s. Eight years before the beginning of the movie, she was persuaded to refuse the proposal of Captain Wentworth, a naval officer with no fortune, despite her love for him. Anne's family has come on hard times, and Wentworth, now wealthy, comes back into her life. Circumstances conspire to keep Anne and Wentworth apart, but eventually love prevails.

Discussion Starter Questions:
✿ Anne was an almost invisible person taken advantage of by others. Was Anne's meek manner admirable? When should women be meek and accommodating? When should we be bold and assertive?

✿ Anne was persuaded not to accept Captain Wentworth's proposal of marriage by a well-meaning friend. How did that counsel affect Anne's life?

✿ As Christian women, how should we evaluate the counsel others give us?

✿ What makes for good counsel? bad counsel?

✿ As Christian women, what should we be mindful of when we counsel others?

MOVIE 13
Snow Falling on Cedars (1999)
Genre: Drama
Length: About 125 minutes
Rating: PG-13

Plot: Set in the Northwest just after World War II, this story tells about a Japanese-American man on trial for the murder of a white fisherman. The white population of the town is openly prejudiced against the Japanese population. The local reporter covering the trial is in love with the accused man's wife; they had been childhood sweethearts, and the reporter had hoped to marry her. The reporter finds evidence of the man's innocence and must decide whether to reveal or conceal it.

Discussion Starter Questions:

✿ The prejudice in this town was very obvious. In real life prejudice can be more subtle. How does prejudice affect our lives and our communities?

✿ Did Hatsue do the right thing when she decided to get married? How did her decision affect the future?

✿ Why did Ishmael have such a hard time deciding to do the right thing?

✿ When in your life have you really struggled to do the right thing? What made it hard? How did things work out? What do you think the rest of Ishmael's life was like?

MOVIE 14
Ever After (1998)
Genre: Romance
Length: About 120 minutes
Rating: PG-13

Plot: This movie is a retelling of the classic Cinderella story. In this version, Danielle, an intelligent, well-read young woman with high ideals, works as a servant to her evil stepmother and stepsisters. Danielle and Prince Henry discuss issues of class structure and destiny as the classic plot unfolds.

Discussion Starter Questions:

✿ When the father dies, he tells his daughter he loves her, but neglects his new wife. How does knowing that we're loved or feeling that we're unloved affect us?

✿ In one scene, Danielle and Prince Henry talk about finding their "destiny." As Christians, we want to find God's will for our lives. How do we find it? How do we know when we've found what God wants for us?

✿ How did this movie deal with themes of envy, injustice, and revenge? Why was the ending so satisfying to us? As Christians, should we be working for justice? Explain.

MOVIE 15
The Secret Garden (1993)

Genre: Children's
Length: About 100 minutes
Rating: G

Plot: Mary Lennox is an orphaned child sent to live with her uncle in England. Left to herself, lonely Mary explores the estate and discovers an abandoned garden. She befriends the brother of one of the maids as well as her crippled cousin, Colin, and together they restore the garden and find friendship and love.

Discussion Starter Questions:

✿ What makes this movie so charming and heartwarming?

✿ The key players in this movie are lonely and wounded people, just like so many people in real life. Why are so many people so lonely?

✿ How did the characters in this movie find healing?

✿ How can people in real life find healing and friendship? How can we help?

MOVIE 16
To Kill a Mockingbird (1962)

Genre: Drama
Length: About 130 minutes
Rating: Not rated

Plot: Atticus Finch, a lawyer in the South during the Depression, is the widowed father of Scout and Jem. Atticus passionately defends a black man who's been wrongly accused of raping a young white woman. Meanwhile, Scout and Jem learn their own lessons about prejudice and acceptance as they interact with their mysterious neighbor Boo Radley.

Discussion Starter Questions:

✿ Why do you think this story is told from Scout's point of view?

✿ In what ways are the story lines about the trial and the mystery and suspicion surrounding Boo Radley related?

✿ Why are we so suspicious of people we don't know or people who are different from us?

✿ How does this relate to the church? Are we as friendly to outsiders as we could be?

✿ How can we guard against prejudice and suspicion?

MOVIE 17
Chicken Run (2000)
Genre: Animated Comedy
Length: About 85 minutes
Rating: G

Plot: This movie tells the story of the chickens at the Tweedy chicken farm. The chickens live in perpetual fear—every hen that doesn't produce eggs is turned into chicken pie. Led by Ginger, a sweet-tempered but determined hen, the chickens dream up an elaborate plan of escape and enlist the services of Rocky the Rooster to help.

Discussion Starter Questions:

✿ The chickens are in a bad situation, but they've formed tight friendships. How does adversity bring us together?

✿ The chickens put a lot of hope and faith in Rocky. Was their hope misplaced? Explain.

✿ When have you been disappointed when you put your hope in someone else? Why is that feeling so awful?

✿ How did Rocky redeem himself?

✿ Ginger ended up motivating and leading the chickens to escape. How did Ginger end up in this leadership role?

✿ What can we learn about leadership from Ginger's example?

MOVIE 18
Driving Miss Daisy (1989)
Genre: Drama
Length: About 100 minutes
Rating: PG

Plot: Set in Georgia, the story begins in 1948 when Miss Daisy, an older and affluent Jewish woman, is made to understand that she is no longer able to drive a car safely. Her son hires a black chauffeur for her. Miss Daisy is resistant to the idea but eventually gives in. The story shows the relationship between Miss Daisy and her chauffeur grow and develop over the next twenty-five years.

Discussion Starter Questions:

✿ Why is Miss Daisy so resistant to the idea of a driver? What made her so testy?

✿ How has prejudice affected Miss Daisy as well as Hoke?

✿ What about growing older bothered Miss Daisy? Why is growing old difficult for people, especially in our culture?

✿ How can we help and support those around us who are growing older?

MOVIE 19
Bruce Almighty (2003)
Genre: Comedy
Length: About 100 minutes
Rating: PG-13

Plot: Bruce Nolan is a frustrated television news reporter doing fluffy human-interest pieces in Buffalo, New York. Nothing in his life is going according to his plans, and he's angry with God. God temporarily gives Bruce his powers while he goes on vacation. Bruce eventually learns that God alone has the right and the ability to run his life and the rest of the world.

Discussion Starter Questions:

✿ Why is Bruce angry with God? Is it OK to be angry with God?

✿ What does Bruce eventually learn about God's nature, his power, and his sovereignty?

✿ What were you thinking when Bruce humbled himself and submitted to God?

✿ How was Bruce's life different at the end of the movie? Was it realistic? What happens when we submit to God?

MOVIE 20
The Good Girl (2002)

Genre: Drama

Length: About 95 minutes

Rating: R

Note: This movie contains graphic scenes. It is not appropriate for every group.
In fact, you'll want to screen this movie before showing it to a group of women.
It's included here because the spiritual lessons are very profound.

Plot: Justine is in a dead-end job in a dead-end town. She finds her childless marriage to a marijuana-smoking husband unfulfilling. She falls into a friendship with Holden, a co-worker who feels as ill-treated as she does. One thing leads to another, and she finds herself having an affair with him. Things quickly spiral downward until Justine finds herself trapped in a dangerous situation. Pay particular attention to Justine's Christian co-worker who encourages her to attend a Bible study at his church.

Discussion Starter Questions:

✿ Justine is dissatisfied with her life. What has led to her dissatisfaction, and how does that dissatisfaction get her in trouble?

✿ How is Justine's dissatisfaction typical of what many women feel? Why are so many women disappointed with life?

✿ What happened when Justine went to church? How many people do you think flirt with the idea of coming to God but then turn away in shame? How can we, the church, help bring them to God?

✿ How does the downward spiral of Justine's life show how sin traps and ensnares us?

✿ How does Justine find grace in the end? Did you find the ending satisfying as a Christian? What was satisfying? What was missing?

✿ What other spiritual lessons did you learn from this movie?

MOVIE 21
Waking Ned Devine (1998)
Genre: Comedy
Length: About 90 minutes
Rating: PG

Plot: Ned Devine has won the lottery—and died from the shock of it. His friends and neighbors decide to have someone impersonate him in order to claim the prize.

Discussion Starter Questions:

✿ What would you do if you won the lottery or inherited a great deal of money? Why do so many people dream about suddenly acquiring money?

✿ What made this movie so charming?

✿ What did you think about the character in the movie who is displeased about her law-breaking neighbors? Was she just a stick-in-the-mud? Is it ever OK to bend the rules like this?

✿ How do friendship and community triumph in this movie? What can we learn from that?

MOVIE 22
Mrs. Brown (1997)
Genre: Drama
Length: About 105 minutes
Rating: PG

Plot: Queen Victoria is in mourning after the death of her beloved husband, Prince Albert. Her outspoken servant, John Brown, helps her through her grief and becomes a trusted friend to the amazement and disapproval of Queen Victoria's family and advisers.

Discussion Starter Questions:

✿ How did John Brown help the queen? How can we help those who are hurting or grieving?

✿ Did you find the relationship between Queen Victoria and John Brown satisfying or disturbing? Why?

✿ Was the reaction of the Queen's family, her advisers, and the other servants appropriate? Why or why not?

✿ In the church, when should we express our opinions about other people's relationships and friendships? When should we keep our opinions to ourselves?

MOVIE 23
Bedazzled (2000)
Genre: Comedy
Length: About 95 minutes
Rating: PG-13

Plot: Elliot is a nerdy office worker who loves Alison from afar. After a humiliating encounter with her, he says he'd give his soul for her. The devil (Elizabeth Hurley) appears and buys his soul in exchange for seven wishes. Things go terribly wrong as Elliot is granted wish after wish.

Discussion Starter Questions:

✿ Elliot's desperate enough to sell his soul to the devil for seven wishes. In real life, what causes people to get involved with things they shouldn't?

✿ Elizabeth Hurley makes a very different devil than what is normally seen in the movies. What about this portrayal of Satan seems accurate? inaccurate?

✿ In real life, how does Satan work to tempt us?

✿ In the movie, the devil didn't exactly tell the truth. What lies does Satan tell us, and why do we fall for them?

✿ How can we resist Satan's ploys?

MOVIE 24
Tuck Everlasting (2002)
Genre: Drama

Length: About 90 minutes

Rating: PG

Plot: Winnie, a teenage girl living in the early 1900s, feels stifled in her upper-class world. While walking in the woods, she discovers Jesse Tuck, a boy from a family with an amazing secret. The Tuck family has discovered a spring with water that gives everlasting life.

Discussion Starter Questions:

✿ What makes Winnie so dissatisfied with her life? When do we feel dissatisfied with the lives we live? How do we seek escape?

✿ What about the Tucks' way of life seems attractive? What's the downside?

✿ What parallels do you see between this story and the story of the woman at the well and the "living water" Jesus offers her? What makes this story different?

✿ What is the cost for "drinking" from the well of living water that Christ offers us? Why is it so difficult for people to leave their old lives behind and choose Christ?

MOVIE 25
The Women (1939)
Genre: Comedy
Length: About 135 minutes
Rating: Not rated

Plot: This classic movie is about a group of society women in New York in the 1930s. Mary Haines discovers her husband is having an affair with Crystal Allen, a cosmetics clerk at an upscale department store. Mary eventually travels to Reno to get a divorce, while her friends ruthlessly gossip about her. But that's not the end of the story—Mary stages an amazing comeback. This timeless movie, with a 130-member, all-woman cast, shows the cattiness, competitiveness, and resilience of women.

Discussion Starter Questions
✿ Does it surprise you that this movie was made more than sixty years ago? In what ways is it still relevant today?

✿ How did Mary handle her heartbreak? How do women survive difficult times today?

✿ Do you think women were portrayed accurately in this movie? Explain.

✿ Mary's friends were not exactly true friends. How did they fall short?

✿ We are a group of women friends, and we are Christians. How can we be real, Christlike friends to each other?

OTHER GREAT CHOICES

Angela's Ashes

Rated R for sexual content and language. Screen this movie first to make sure it's appropriate for your group.

The story of a poverty-stricken, mixed-faith family in the 1930s and 1940s Ireland. As Frank, a son, grows up, he begins to see the truth about his family and realizes that he can rise above poverty and despair. Use this movie to talk about hope and despair and what it takes to overcome trials.

Anna and the King

RATED PG-13

This is the nonmusical version of *The King and I*. In 1860 Anna goes to Siam to be tutor to the King's children. The movie explores differences between East and West, the influence of women, and gender roles. Use this movie to talk about gender roles in today's society as well as how women can influence those around them for good.

The Apostle

RATED PG-13

This is the story of a far-from-perfect minister in the south who searches for redemption after committing an act of violence. He forms a new church and his ministry thrives until the law catches up with him. Use this movie to talk about Christian morality, remorse, grace, and forgiveness.

Bend It Like Beckham

RATED PG-13

This movie is about a teenage girl who wants to be a soccer star although it's against the wishes of her conservative Indian parents. Use this movie to talk about honoring one's parents and about fulfilling one's dreams.

Charlotte's Web

RATED G

This is the classic animated children's movie. Charlotte, a wise spider, saves the life of Wilber the pig. Use this movie to talk about friendship, self-sacrifice, and love.

Cold Comfort Farm
RATED PG

Miss Flora Poste finds herself orphaned and without enough money to live in 1930s England. She moves in with eccentric relatives and changes their lives for the better. Use this movie to talk about family relations and also about being an influence in others' lives.

The Count of Monte Cristo
RATED PG-13

Edmond Dantes is betrayed by a friend and wrongly imprisoned. After thirteen years, he escapes and undertakes an elaborate plan for revenge. Use this movie to talk about being falsely accused and revenge.

The Legend of Bagger Vance
RATED PG-13

Rannulph Junuh is a disillusioned golfer who's lost his swing. Bagger Vance, Junuh's caddy, helps him find himself again. Use this movie to talk about overcoming obstacles and disappointments. You may also want to use this movie to talk about how the Holy Spirit guides us.

Les Misérables
RATED PG-13

A classic story of revenge and redemption. Jean Valjean is imprisoned for two decades for stealing a loaf of bread. After his release, he rebuilds his life but finds his crime follows him. Use this movie to talk about redemption and grace.

Liar, Liar
RATED PG-13

Jim Carrey plays a lawyer who can't tell a lie for twenty-four hours. Use this movie to talk about the lies that grown-ups tell and the importance of honesty.

Lilies of the Field
NOT RATED

This classic from 1963 features Sidney Poitier as a traveler who stops at a mission to get water for his overheated car. The nuns think he is sent by God to build a chapel. Use this movie to talk about faith and friendship. You can also use this movie to talk about how the Holy Spirit directs our lives.

Pay It Forward
RATED PG-13

Seventh-grader Trevor McKinney's social-studies teacher gives his class an assignment: do something to change the world. Trevor's idea is to do something "big" for three people, who would each then do something big for another three people. Watch how this idea plays out in the movie. Then talk about the how it compares to the golden rule.

The Prime of Miss Jean Brodie
RATED PG

Miss Brodie is a Scottish teacher at an all-girls school in the 1930s. Miss Brodie has strong opinions, and she influences her students profoundly. Use this movie to talk about how others influence us and how we influence others. Also talk about the strengths and weaknesses in Miss Brodie's character and the need for discernment when dealing with those in positions of authority over us.

The Truman Show
RATED PG

It's the ultimate reality show. Truman Burbank's life is a television show, and he's the only one who doesn't know it. Truman's family, his friends, and everyone in his town are all hired actors. The show is directed by Christof, a man who causes the sun to rise every morning. Slowly, Truman becomes aware of his situation. Use this movie to talk about free will. Discuss how God can be in control of the world while people still have free will. Discuss how God is different from the director Christof.

What About Bob?
RATED PG

Dr. Leo Marvin is a psychiatrist who acquires a very needy patient named Bob. Bob is afraid of everything and clings to Dr. Marvin, even following him on his family vacation, where absolutely everything goes wrong. Use this movie to talk about how we Christians are to treat those who get on our nerves.✿

section **six**

celebrations AND SPECIAL EVENTS

Every good women's ministry includes celebrations and special events. There are occasions in all women's lives that call for a little something extra.

You'll see that the ideas in this section are varied. There are community events, family events, parties, holiday events, and more. Some are one-time or seasonal events that will require a lot of preparation and planning. Be sure to give your team plenty of time to get ready.

Other ideas in this section may be events that you'll want to plan to do every year. Each year women will look forward to these events with great anticipation. You'll find that the first year will take the most planning. After that, you'll be able re-create the event each succeeding year based on the same format. Be sure to add in a little something new every year, though, so that your events don't become stale and predictable.

There are several events in this section that are designed to celebrate family relationships or a special time in someone's life. No matter how big your women's ministry gets, don't neglect to offer events that will celebrate new marriages, new babies, and other joyous times in women's lives.

You'll find that many of these events would make wonderful outreach events. Please use them as such. You'll also find that many of the events would work well for women who'd like to join forces with the other churches in their area. All women who trust in Christ's death and resurrection are sisters, so don't shy away from working in community with the other women's ministry teams in your area. You have much to gain from the cooperation.

You'll also find wonderful ideas in this section for worship and other large-group events designed to help women experience God in their lives. Don't forget to plan time not only to learn about God but also to celebrate his goodness, his faithfulness, and his lovingkindness. This is the grandest of all "special events"!

IDEA 1
quilt show

Do women in your church make or collect lovely quilts? Host a quilt show to display these beautiful works of art. Invite women from the church and the community to view the quilts.

Several weeks before the event, ask the women in your church to sign up to display their quilts. Plan to display the quilts in a room with tall ceilings or to drape each quilt over a banquet table.

Have each quilt owner write on a display card where the quilt comes from, when it was made, who made it, what the quilt pattern is, and any other interesting information about the quilt.

Ask quilt owners to be available during the event to answer questions about their quilts. Ask the attendees not to touch the quilts, or pass out white cotton gloves so the quilts don't become soiled.

Invite quilters to give demonstrations on piecing and quilting techniques. You may want to offer a quilting class at the church that any interested women can attend.

Have information about the care of quilts available. Generally, heirloom quilts should be wrapped in acid-free tissue paper, folded loosely, and stored away from light, heat, and excessive humidity or dryness. Quilts that are used every day will last longer if they are dry-cleaned or hand-washed and air-dried. Wet quilts should never be wrung dry. All quilts should be kept out of bright sunlight so they don't fade.

Be sure to have information about your church's women's ministry programs available as well.

IDEA 2
variety night

Organize a variety night featuring the talents of women who attend your church. Encourage women to sign up to do poetry readings, sing or play an instrument, present skits, juggle, do acrobatics, tell jokes, or do any other kind of performance. Who knows what kinds of hidden talents you'll discover?

Invite the rest of the women in the church to come to this just-for-fun event. This is a great chance for women to invite their neighbors or co-workers for a girl's night out.

IDEA 3
arts festival

Chances are there are many artistic women in your church. Provide an opportunity for these women to display their talents during an all-day arts festival. Invite all artistic women to take part. You may find women who sew, knit, crochet, embroider, weave, quilt, do pottery, paint watercolors, or create crafts.

Encourage each woman to bring lots of samples of her work and set up a booth. Have the women plan to be working on one of their projects during the event. This means you'll need to make arrangements for the potters to bring their pottery wheels and for the quilters to set up their quilting racks or sewing machines.

Invite everyone in your church to come and see the wonderful variety of artistic expression. Encourage all the artists to give demonstrations of their crafts. Some women may want to provide supplies so that the attendees can try their hand at the art. For example, quilters may allow people to take a few stitches. Potters may provide clay for hand-building. Painters may set up extra easels with canvasses or paper.

Enjoy this just-for-fun event, and have fun getting to know the women in your church better. You may also want to have the artists provide classes later to those interested in learning how to do each kind of art.

IDEA 4
mother-and-son tea

Hold a formal tea for moms and their sons. Use formal, but not frilly, decorations. For example, use dark blue or dark green tablecloths. Use fresh flowers in bright, primary colors—no pinks or lavenders.

Send an invitation by mail to each mom with a son. You may want to include a list of etiquette rules with the invitations to help everyone get ready to practice his or her manners. Rules might include: a gentleman always holds the lady's chair while she's being seated, gentlemen never take more than two cookies, gentleman fold their napkins neatly over one knee and use their napkins instead of their sleeves to wipe their mouths.

Have people come in their best clothes. Serve tea, cakes, cookies, and sandwiches on real china. Invite several of the moms and their sons to provide special music or short skits. You may want to provide table discussion topics to help moms and sons practice making polite conversation with others. Choose topics that boys might be interested in. Some of the topics can be serious and others silly. For example, you may want to have moms and sons talk about their favorite vacation, their favorite sport, or their favorite bug. Encourage the moms and sons to listen politely while others talk and to show their interest in what others are saying by asking polite follow-up questions.

IDEA 5
mother-and-son fishing derby

Make arrangements at a local fishpond to have a fishing-derby event for moms and sons.

Usually such ponds are stocked with fish so there are plenty of fish to be caught. Some places will provide tackle, poles, and bait.

Arrange for the staff at the fishpond to give everyone a quick lesson on how to use a fishing pole and how to bait the hook. Then have the moms and sons spend a couple hours fishing. Offer prizes for the biggest fish, the most fish, the smallest fish, and the prettiest or ugliest fish.

After the derby, enjoy a fish fry together. Serve fried fish, french fries, and coleslaw. Have cookies for dessert.

IDEA 6
marriage 101

Holding individual bridal showers can be time-consuming and expensive. Instead, host an annual event to celebrate new marriages. Once a year, invite engaged women, newly married women, and their mothers to this all-day Saturday event.

Open with coffee, prayer, and worship. Then invite all of the attendees to go to small elective classes on running a household, budgets and debt, decorating, cooking, praying with your husband, and relatives and stepfamilies. Find women in your church to teach these seminars. All of the classes should include group discussion and prayer. Also, each class should include handouts that fit into a notebook so the women have the information for future reference.

At noon, bring the women together for lunch and a short program with door prizes (the centerpieces). Offer the small elective classes again in the afternoon. End the afternoon by serving typical bridal-shower fare: cake, mixed nuts, mints, and punch.

IDEA 7
bridal and baby gifts

Giving gifts to new wives or new moms can get very expensive, and it can be time-consuming to do all that shopping. Still, it's nice to recognize these special events in women's lives. Consider purchasing appropriate books in bulk (so you can get a discount) and giving each woman the same gift when she celebrates her special day.

IDEA 8
wedding china

This is a great idea for a bridal shower or for any other formal dinner event.

Ask all of the married women in your church to bring in two place settings of their wedding china before the event. One place setting will be for the woman who brings that china; the other will be for a single woman or a guest. This idea is especially fun if your group includes older women whose wedding china is several decades old. If there are single women in your group with formal or heirloom china, invite them to bring in their pieces as well. Be very careful to label each woman's china so that nothing gets lost.

Set the tables with the china. During the event, invite all the women to tour the room and look at all of the beautiful place settings. Then have the women sit down at their own china. Guests or women who didn't bring china can sit at the extra place settings.

Serve the food buffet-style.

Have a team of responsible volunteers carefully hand wash all of the china after the dinner.

IDEA 9
formal night

Hold a formal dinner at your church one evening, and have the meal catered.

Invite women to wear formal gowns to the dinner. Women might wear old bridesmaid dresses, prom dresses, or other formal gowns that they own. Other women may want to check out local thrift stores for inexpensive formals.

If you can, have a red carpet available at the entrance to the room. Decorate the tables elegantly with cloth tablecloths and napkins, and use fresh flowers as centerpieces.

You may want to use the "God's Princesses" devotion on page 75 for the program at this event.

IDEA 10
weddings gone by

One of the best ways your women's ministry can help to develop friendships among women of different ages is through a bridal fashion show. Invite all the women of the church to come.

Arrange the tables in the room to create a "runway." Arrange for traditional wedding music to be played. Give engaged women and newly married women seats of honor right on the runway.

For the fashion show, invite the older women in your church to wear their wedding dresses or to donate them for the day for someone else to wear. You can also borrow vintage gowns from local museums. Women who got married during those eras can narrate descriptions of the gowns and might describe some of the wedding practices from those times.

Have an old-fashioned reception to complete the event, and be sure to serve wedding cake.

IDEA 11
money seminars

Once a year, plan an event to teach women how to handle money. This event would be very beneficial for single women who are just starting out, for teens, and for anyone who would like to learn more about money.

Invite older women or women who work in the financial world to teach classes on topics such as saving money, learning to tithe, stocks and bonds, getting out of debt, and planning for large purchases. Make sure all the classes are taught from a biblical perspective.

IDEA 12
holiday homes tour

A holiday homes tour is a great way for women with the gift of hospitality to use their gifts.

Set up a tour of homes belonging to women in your women's ministry. Ask several women who enjoy decorating for the holidays to open their homes for the tour. Encourage the women to decorate around a theme and to include decorations that point to their faith in Christ. You may want to have an overall theme for the tour: for example, Homes That Light the Way.

The hostesses can act as living witnesses of God's grace and love through their gracious welcome of others into their homes. Encourage hostesses to provide some sort of light refreshment, such as mulled cider and a cookie tray.

A home that's open for the tour might also display another woman's collection. For example, perhaps someone in your group has collected nutcrackers, bears, or nativity scenes from around the world.

You can sell tickets at a very reasonable price to make your home tour more affordable than the tours hosted by other organizations. The holiday home tour is a fantastic way to raise money to use for scholarships for other women's ministry functions. It's also a wonderful, nonthreatening event for women to invite their non-Christian friends to.

IDEA 13
worship services

Plan these worship services to meet the needs of women who want a longer, more concentrated time of corporate prayer and worship. Have the worship service last for two to three hours on a Saturday morning, and structure the time around corporate praise, singing, worship, individual prayer and journaling, and prayer in groups of three or four. Be sure to have a blank journal available for each woman at these events. When it's time to journal, play quiet music in the background, and encourage all the women to find a spot where they can be by themselves to reflect on God's work in their lives.

You might organize each worship service around a theme. Here are some ideas:

quilts of prayer
Hold this service outside on the grassy or shady areas of your church grounds or go to a park. Spread quilts, comforters, and blankets on the ground. Encourage the women to dress casually and to get comfortable on the quilts. Have the women pray corporately about specific topics and then break into groups of three for personal sharing and prayer. You may want to end this event with a fellowship picnic. Have all the women bring a picnic lunch, or provide buckets of chicken with potato salad and coleslaw.

marriage feast of the lamb
Decorate the sanctuary of your church for an elaborate wedding. Use personal, wedding-style invitations to invite women to attend. The invitations can be passed out during the weekly worship service two weeks prior to the event. On the day of the service, use your church's candelabras and decorate with fresh flowers and pew bows. At the

front of the room, use a floral arch and perhaps even a padded kneeler. Behind the kneeler, place communion elements on a table. You may want to include an aisle runner too. Begin with a time of worship, singing, and directed prayer. Then explain the symbolism of the church as the bride of Christ. Invite the women to walk reverently up the aisle and take communion before returning to their seats for a time of personal reflection and prayer.

harvest of praise

Decorate the sanctuary with pumpkins, gourds, fall leaves, and baskets of corn. You may find a local farmer who would be glad to rent his pumpkins for a single day. Choose Scriptures and songs that focus on thankfulness and praise. If the day is warm enough, send the women outside to enjoy the briskness of fall and to observe the changes that are happening in creation on a crisp fall day. Encourage the women to pray outside. This would be a great time to have women take turns telling the others what God has done for them. You can make this into an "open mic" opportunity. Invite women to come to the microphone as God leads them and tell why they're thankful.

prayer walk

Use Christmas lights to mark a path for prayer in your sanctuary. It's easiest if you have a room that doesn't have pews, but it's also possible to work around the pews. The path should wind through the entire room. Keep the overhead lighting as dim as possible—not so dim that people will be in danger of tripping, but dim enough to create an atmosphere of quiet reverence. You may want to have very soft, calm music playing in the background. Gregorian chants or instrumental hymn arrangements are good choices. Create these ten stations along the path:

✿ At the first station, put a pen and a tablet of paper. Write "To Do" on the tablet in large, bold letters. Put an instruction card at this station that says, "We come with the cares of the world weighing heavy on our minds. There's so much to do. Write down your most pressing to-do tasks, and leave them here. Prepare to enter God's peace and rest your weary soul.

✿ At the next station, put a basket of apples, a stack of inexpensive note cards, pens, and tape. Make an instruction card for this station that says, "You're about to meet with a holy, perfect God who sees all and knows all. This is no place for harbored, secret sin. Make a clean breast of it: Confess your sins to God, and turn from them. Write them on a card, and seal the card with tape. Place the cards under the basket. Thank God for the forgiveness he's given you."

✿ At the next station, place a stack of magazines with themes that would distract women from following God. Also display a large, pink, poster-board heart, and have pens available. Include an instruction card that says, "There is much that distracts us from following our first love. Consider what's pulling you away from God. Refocus your heart on God, and let love for him flow through you. Tell God why you love him. Write something on the heart that will represent your commitment to love God."

✿ Place a tabletop fountain at the next station. (You'll need access to an electrical outlet.) Place a basket of small pebbles by the fountain. Include an instruction card that says, "God offers peace and joy. The song says that we can have peace like a river and joy like a fountain. Pick up a pebble, and hold it in your hand. Consider your life. How is it lacking in peace and joy? Ask God to give you his peace, his joy. Place your pebble in the fountain. Feel God's peace wash over you as you listen to the quiet burble of the fountain. Praise God for his peace. Respond to God in joy."

✿ Place a basket of delectable candies on the table at the next station and include a small bowl for candy wrappers. The instruction card at this station should say, "The Word says, 'Taste and see that the Lord is good.' Place a piece of candy on your tongue, and savor the taste. As the candy melts in your mouth, dwell on how the Lord is good."

✿ At this point, the path should lead to the platform in your sanctuary. Place a simple cross here. Place communion elements on the table. Having only one cup will be a powerful symbol of community. You may need to have someone available to refill the cup occasionally. Place a card here that says, "Christ calls us to oneness—oneness with him and oneness with each other. His spirit lives within us. All who believe in him are one body. Remember him as you take the bread. Recommit to the new covenant as you drink from the cup. Feel God's Spirit within you. Linger here, praising God for his gift. Linger here, experiencing the belonging that comes from being one with Christ and his church. You are loved. You are his."

❀ Place several very small, very clear bells at the next station. Include an instruction card that says, "Sing this song in your mind, or simply pray the words if you don't know the tune:

'Praise God, from whom all blessings flow;

Praise him, all creatures here below;

Allelujah, Allelujah!

Praise him above, ye heav'nly host;

Praise Father, Son, and Holy Ghost.

Allelujah, Allelujah

Allelujah, Allelujah

Allelujah!'

"Now praise God! Tell God why he is praiseworthy, and bask in his glory. For each praiseworthy thing you mention, gently and joyfully ring the bell."

❀ At this station, place a beautifully gift-wrapped box. Place an instruction card nearby that says, "Sing this song in your mind, or simply pray the words if you don't know the tune:

'Breathe on me, breath of God.

Fill me with life anew,

That I may love what thou dost love,

And do what thou wouldst do.'

Welcome the Holy Spirit's changing presence in your life. Offer yourself to God. Thank God for the gift of the Holy Spirit. And thank God for the gifts of the Spirit that he's granted you. Receive this gift, open it, and use it."

❀ At the next station, place a church directory and a bucket of blocks, such as LEGO blocks. Use a few of the blocks to begin building a house. The instruction card at this station should say, "Soon you will re-enter the world. You will meet God's people. God calls us to love, to serve, to build up, to encourage, to make disciples. With your mind's eye, see the people you will meet. Ask God to grow your love for them, to show you where they need help and encouragement. God's Word says that we who believe are 'like living stones… being built into a spiritual house.' Add your block to the building. Then add a few more blocks to represent those you will encourage and disciple."

❀ A this station, place another large notebook with "To Do" in large, bold letters. Include an instruction card that says, "It's time to join the world again. Consider how you have changed during this experience. What will you do? What seems most pressing now? Pause for God's guidance. Write your new to dos on the list. Then prepare to enter the world."

IDEA 14
mother-and-teenage-daughter tea

At least once a year, host a mother and daughter tea to help open up the lines of communication between mothers and their teenage daughters.

Before the event, arrange for several mothers and daughters to be on a panel to discuss issues of concern for moms and daughters. Ask them tough questions such as,

- How do you resist peer pressure?
- How do you get along with your mom [or daughter]?
- How do you resolve differences of opinion about curfews, dating, and other issues?
- What's the most challenging part of being a daughter [or mom]?

Encourage the moms and daughters to keep talking about these topics at home.

IDEA 15
mother-and-young-daughter tea

This is a wonderful opportunity for daughters to practice their party manners.

Hold a tea for mothers and their young daughters. Invite all the guests to wear their best dresses, hats, and gloves. And encourage all the daughters to bring their favorite stuffed animals and their favorite books.

Decorate the room with pretty tablecloths, fresh flowers, and beautiful paper plates and cups. Use frilly paper doilies for place mats.

Plan a table setting for each mother, each daughter, and each stuffed animal. Provide tables where the girls can display their books.

Before the tea is served, invite all the mothers and girls to look at all the books on display and to "meet" one another's stuffed animals.

Then serve warm herbal tea with dainty cookies and mini-muffins.

Arrange for a few of the young girls who are taking piano lessons to provide the special music.

IDEA 16
mother-and-daughter pajama party

Invite moms and their daughters to come to a pajama party. It's best if you plan the party either for elementary-age daughters or for teenage daughters, rather than trying to have both ages at the same party.

Have everyone come in pajamas, slippers, and robe. Play silly games. For example, do this pillowcase relay:

Form teams of six. Have each team line up for a relay race. At the other end of the room, place several large pillows and pillowcases. You'll need one pillow and pillowcase for each team.

On go, the first person in each team should run to the other side of the room, put a pillowcase on the pillow, and run back to the line carrying the pillow. The second person on each team should then take the pillow back across the room, take the pillow out of the pillowcase, and return empty-handed to her line. The third person on each team should run across the room, put the pillowcase back on the pillow, and run back to the line carrying the pillow. The race is over when the sixth person has run across the room and taken the pillowcase off of the pillow.

Later, set out the ingredients for banana splits, and have each mom and daughter build a huge banana split to share. Then watch a fun movie, such as *Mary Poppins*, before ending the party.

IDEA 17
christmas repast

Hold a Christmas banquet every year, and invite women to come with their non-Christian friends, co-workers, and neighbors. This banquet can easily be a breakfast or a luncheon instead of a dinner. For many women, it's much easier to schedule in a brunch banquet during this busy time.

Have the meal catered unless you have a fabulous team of cooks in your church. You may want to ask the men in your church to be the table servers. Invite a speaker to talk about the spiritual meaning of the Christmas holiday. Have talented musicians from your church offer the special music. End the meal with a clear invitation about how to become a Christian. Here are some themes:

gifts from the heart

Decorate the tables with green, red, and purple tablecloths. For centerpieces, stack heart-shaped red, green, and purple boxes. Have the speaker focus her talk on the gift that God has given us, and the gifts of the heart we can give to one another during this season and around the year. If you're serving a luncheon, you may want to serve petits fours that are decorated to look like gift boxes.

wonders of his love

Decorate the tables with blue and silver tablecloths. Hang giant snowflakes from the ceiling and on the walls. Make snowflakes from doilies to scatter on the tables. Use stuffed snowmen and miniature Christmas trees as centerpieces. You may want to dress some children as "snow babies" Have them wear white, and attach glittering poster-board snowflakes to their backs. They can "whiz" through the room on rollerblades and deliver small gift bags containing women's ministry information to each woman. Have a speaker with a dramatic testimony tell of the wonders of God's love for her.

an heirloom christmas

Decorate the tables with burgundy and cream tablecloths. Use piles of evergreen boughs, pinecones, and garlands of pearls for the centerpieces. This would be an excellent time to invite the women in your church to bring in heirloom ornaments. You can display these on each table. Have the speaker talk about the legacy of faith that we have received from those who have gone before us.

ornaments of praise

Decorate the tables with red and green tablecloths. Use clear bowls or cake plates piled high with glass Christmas ornaments as the centerpieces. Place a Christmas tree at the front of the room. Ask each woman to bring an ornament for a gift exchange. Have the women hang their ornaments on the tree. Have the speaker talk about how our praise honors God in the same way that ornaments grace a tree.

Have the women draw numbers and take turns choosing an ornament from the tree.

IDEA 18
garden tours

This is a great idea to use as an outreach idea or a fundraiser.

Plan to have this event during the season of the year when local gardens will be looking their best. Find five to seven women in your group who have lovely gardens. It's best if the gardens are not too far apart.

Invite women to come and bring their friends, co-workers, or family members.

Put together packets of information to give to each attendee. The packets should include a map to each garden, a description of each garden, and a short bio of the gardener. Also include information about the hours for the event. For example, the gardens could be available for viewing in any order between 10 a.m. and 3 p.m. You will also want to include some information about the other women's ministry programs that your church offers.

You may also want to have a garden boutique and sell handcrafted items and unusual plants. Some of the featured gardeners may want to offer seeds or plant slips from their gardens.

You could also invite several gardeners from your church to offer mini-workshops on gardening in your area. Gardeners could address soil improvements and pest control, as well as tips on plants that thrive in your area.

You may also want to have one garden set up for tea. Choose a large garden, and scatter tables throughout. Provide tea and lemonade with homemade cookies, scones, and sandwiches. Be sure to have a team of women to serve the tea. You may want to only offer tea during one or two hours of the event.

IDEA 19
ladies teas

Teas seem to have universal appeal to women, and they offer opportunities for lots of variety and imagination. Here are several ideas.

• Have several women offer to be table hostesses. These women should bring in their own china, silverware, tablecloths, and centerpieces. If possible, each hostess should also bring her own teapot. Each hostess should then decorate her own table. This is especially fun because every table will be different. Women who love to decorate can have fun decorating their tables as dramatically as they wish.

• Provide a program of special music or skits. You may also want to have a speaker give a special talk. For example, perhaps the speaker could talk about biblical womanhood. Just having a speaker share her testimony is also a great idea.

• Serve tea and provide cream, sugar, and fresh lemon slices. Also provide scones, homemade cookies, and party sandwiches. At a fancy tea, you may also want to serve petits fours or deviled eggs.

• Plan a theme tea party. Decorating around a special theme can add to the fun. Here are some ideas:

His Paintbrush, His Palette—Decorate with bright colors and painting supplies. Have the speaker talk about God's creativity at work in our lives.

Legacy of a Thankful Heart—Decorate with fall colors. Invite several women to tell what God's done for them.

Love Stories—Decorate with red, pink, and white. Invite missionaries to tell how God's love is making a difference in the world.

Making Memories—Decorate with photos and scrapbook albums. Invite women to talk about their memories of childhood or school. Invite all the women to bring a special photo to share with the other women at their tables. The speaker can talk about how our memories affect our lives for good and bad.

Back to the Future—This is a great theme for a graduation tea. Invite high school or college graduates to attend with their mothers. Decorate with mortarboards and wrapped "diplomas." Have the speaker talk about the wonderful opportunities God plans for our future.

MORE IDEAS FOR TEAS

✿ **Hat Tea**—Invite everyone to come wearing a favorite hat.
✿ **BYOC**—Have everyone bring their own favorite teacup and saucer and be ready to tell the other women why it's their favorite.

- ✿ **Costume Tea**—Invite all the women to come dressed as their favorite woman from history.
- ✿ **Prayer Tea**—Give a sheet of prayer requests to each table, and have the women pray for others after they've enjoyed their tea.
- ✿ **Neighborhood Tea**—Have several women host teas in their neighborhoods. Neighborhood teas can be a great way for women to get to know their neighbors and eventually invite them to come to church.
- ✿ **New Member Tea**—Invite the new women in your group to come to a tea to get to know one another. Also invite women who've been a part of your church for quite a while so that half of the attendees can offer hospitality and friendship to the new women.
- ✿ **If We Were Queen of the World Teas**—Have the women come prepared to talk about an issue or a problem that needs to be solved. For example, perhaps you need to find a way to reach your city for Christ, or maybe you need to find a way to provide support for a particular missionary. After enjoying tea, have the women brainstorm ways to solve the problem. Together, choose the best ideas and implement them.

IDEA 20
spiritual birthday party

Celebrate spiritual growth in your group by having a spiritual birthday party once a year.

Provide birthday cake and ice cream. Put one candle on the cake for each woman represented by your women's ministry.

Give a brief talk about how each year spent with Christ brings spiritual growth. Light the candles, and then have the women's ministry leadership team blow them out. Have everyone take a piece of cake and some ice cream.

Then have each table of women share with one another what the year has brought them. Have them discuss their trials and their triumphs and what God has taught them through it all.

It would be wonderful to hold this event every year. As women anticipate and participate in this event annually, they'll begin to really pay attention to the big picture of what God is doing in their lives or in their friends' lives.

This is also a wonderful way to end each year of women's ministry programs. You may want to provide each woman with a spiritual birthday gift: a Christian book to read. If your group takes a hiatus over the summer, at least you'll know that you have provided a way for women to continue their spiritual discoveries during that time. Giving all the women the same book to read will also provide a sense of community.

IDEA 21
in-home recitals

 Does your group include women with musical talents? Hold several in-home recitals as a way to get small groups of women together during the year.

Enlist one or two women to provide several selections of special music, either classical or sacred, for the occasion. (About twenty minutes of music would be about right.) Have these women also be prepared to share stories about their relationship with Christ.

Invite small groups of women to attend each event. Present the music first, have the women tell their stories, then provide refreshments and time for the women to simply enjoy getting to know one another better.

This is a great way to invite neighbors and friends to a church event.

IDEA 22
praise night

 Have a women-only night of praise at your church. Invite the worship team from your church to provide at least an hour (or maybe two!) of praise music. And be sure to provide child care.

Invite the women to come and praise God together in song. Don't plan for a teaching time—just sing praises to God. Plan to include a variety of music according to the tastes of the women at your church. Some groups may want hymns and choruses. Others may want to sing only choruses.

Enjoy a sweet time of praise together! You may want to hold this event in your church's sanctuary, but you could also meet in a local park or on the lawn outside your church building.

Praise Night would be an excellent event to invite the women from a sister church to attend.

IDEA 23
maundy thursday meal

Few churches celebrate Maundy Thursday anymore. Hold this worship service for the women in your church, or host a church-wide event.

Have the women in your church prepare a simple soup-and-bread meal to be shared together by candlelight. When the meal is over, quickly and quietly clear the tables.

Sing several solemn Easter hymns together such as, "When I Survey the Wondrous Cross," "O Sacred Head, Now Wounded," and "Beneath the Cross of Jesus." Then celebrate communion together, remembering Jesus' last supper with his disciples.

At many churches, a foot-washing service is a traditional part of a Maundy Thursday service. If you'd like to include this in your service, provide a basin of warm water and a towel for each table. Have the women take turns kneeling before another woman and washing her feet. This should be done in quiet contemplation of Christ's humility.

It's also a custom in some churches to take a collection for the poor on Maundy Thursday. If you'd like to do that, put baskets at the back of the room so people can put their donations in as they leave.

At the end of the service, quietly snuff out the candles, and leave the church in silence.

IDEA 24
sunrise service breakfast

Many churches hold a sunrise service on Easter morning in addition to their normal Sunday worship services. Many people plan to attend both services, but may find it inconvenient to go home between services.

Have the women's ministry in your church host a drop-by breakfast for your congregation so that people can drop by between the services to have a bite of breakfast and chat with others to pass the time before the next service. Ask women to prepare Easter delicacies such as hot cross buns and hard-boiled eggs colored with Easter-egg dye.

Set up tables in your church's fellowship hall, and serve the breakfast, including beverages such as orange juice, hot chocolate, and coffee, buffet-style.

Have a team of women on hand to wipe tables, set out more food, and make more coffee. If your church has more than one regular worship service, consider providing the buffet all morning.✿

outreach

The Bible tells us at the end of Matthew that we are to share the good news of Christ and make disciples. This section will help you, and the women in your church, fulfill that commandment.

Women often find it very difficult to share their faith with others. Women, especially Christian women, are taught from childhood to be polite, kind, and gentle. We don't want to offend or to cause dissension or strife.

In this section, you'll find ideas that will help women share their faith joyfully and effectively. You'll also find ideas for events that your women's ministry can sponsor to help draw the community in to your church.

Offer enough of these activities in your programs to make outreach a natural part of what you do. People get better at whatever they practice. It only stands to reason that the more outreach you do, the better your group will be at it and the less people will be afraid of it. The more outreach you do, the more likely it is that your church will develop a true love for people and a passionate desire to introduce them to Christ. Also, the more connected you get to the community through outreach events, the more the community will know your church as a welcoming, friendly, and loving group of Christ followers.

IDEA 1
winter garden party

Host winter garden parties for seniors in your community who are widowed and have no local family.

Hold the parties in individual homes, but have the women's ministry team help the hostess with the planning and purchasing.

Each hostess should invite the senior women in her neighborhood to her party. The hostess, with one or two assistants, should serve the refreshments and give each senior woman the supplies she needs to transplant plant slips into pots. These supplies (the pots, soil, rocks, gloves, plant slips, and other gardening paraphernalia) should be provided by the women's ministry program.

Not only will this event provide new plants for the women during the cold dreary days of winter, but it will also help women find new friends and connect with the community.

IDEA 2
thanksgiving turkey dinner

Plan a community-wide or a neighborhood-wide Thanksgiving dinner, and plan for it to be an annual event. The goal of the Thanksgiving dinner is to build a spirit of community in your neighborhood and good relationships between your church and the community.

Send out fliers at least a couple of weeks in advance of the event. A good time for the dinner would be early November. Price the meal very inexpensively so that people will be compelled to attend—who can resist an inexpensive, home-cooked meal that they don't have to cook themselves? Encourage the community to make reservations for the meal so you know how much food you'll need to provide.

Have the women in your church sign up to donate the food, and encourage the women to cook from scratch as much as possible. You'll need teams of women to coordinate the food donations and the menu, to decorate and set up tables, to welcome people and take their money, to serve the food and beverages, and to clean up afterward. Be sure to designate people to be in charge of the various teams, so that several people share the responsibility. Whatever isn't donated needs to be paid for from the women's ministry budget.

Make sure to have fliers available that describe all of the church's ministries. Provide time (and room) before and after the dinner for fellowship so that community members can spend time getting acquainted.

Consider the event an outreach activity and a service to the community. But the funds can also be used to fund various charities and women's ministry programs at your church.

IDEA 3
community Bible study

Consider starting a Bible study/church service specifically for women who don't attend church. Many women simply do not know anything about Christ. Many others have left the church because they married non-Christians or because they rebelled in their youth. These women may feel out of place or even embarrassed in church. Provide a nonthreatening place where they can learn about God. Plan a simple service with praise and worship, a speaker who can explain practical Christian principles based on God's Word, prayer, refreshments, and fellowship.

Many of these women may find themselves in crisis situations; for example, they may have an abusive spouse, drug and alcohol issues, or legal trouble. In addition to offering these women a chance to study the Bible, gather and display information about Christian and community resources like housing, legal help, counseling, healthcare, food and nutrition services, tutoring, GED or continuing education services, job assistance, and more. Find out how the social service programs in your area work so you can knowledgably help women find the assistance they need.

IDEA 4
pencil evangelism

At the beginning of each new school term, provide a new pen and a new pencil to each school-age child or teenager in your church.

Have the pens and pencils printed with your church's name, address, and phone number and with a Scripture verse. You can count on children to leave their belongings all over, so the pens and pencils will be well distributed in your community. Choose a new color for every school term. Use bright colors on good quality pens and pencils. This project will also help parents a little with the sometimes crippling costs of school supplies.

IDEA 5
visitor gift bags

Prepare special gift bags for women who are new to the group, and have them available at every event.

Include a letter from the women's ministry staff thanking new women for coming to the event. The gift bag should also include a New Testament, a pamphlet that explains how to become a Christian, a small devotional guide, a brochure listing all of the ministries of the women's ministry and the church, and a couple of packets of gourmet hot-chocolate mix. Be sure to also include phone numbers and e-mail addresses of women on your women's ministry staff. Put all of the items in pretty gift bags with pretty tissue paper.

IDEA 6
coffee and chat

Once a month hold an entry-point event at your church building. The event should be an easy, nonthreatening evening that women can invite their non-Christian friends, neighbors, and co-workers to.

Make sure the atmosphere is relaxed, friendly, and very informal, and make sure the regular attendees know that their job is to welcome new women into the group and make friends with them. Welcome each guest warmly.

Serve coffee and a homemade dessert, such as cobbler or pie.

Invite a speaker from outside your church to speak on a nonspiritual topic that would be helpful to anyone. For example, the speaker could talk about nutrition, fitness, simplifying the holidays, investing, or being single in today's world.

IDEA 7
dollar giveaway

Print small invitations to a women's ministry outreach event. Then fold a dollar bill around each invitation so that the invitation isn't visible. Send a team of women to a place where women gather, and have the team drop the prepared dollar bills on the floor for women to find. For example, teams might drop the invitations in the clothing, housewares, or baby section of a department store. Or they might drop the bills at a local bookstore.

IDEA 8
free stuff giveaway

Print small invitations to a women's ministry outreach event and then attach coupons to the invitations. The coupons might be for a free carwash or a free fast-food burger.

Distribute these invitations to women at the mall, in the park, or at local festivals.

IDEA 9
community musicians

Have some of the women musicians in your church work on a program of popular Christian music to present at coffeehouses, bookstores, or shopping malls.

The women should think carefully about the songs they choose to perform; the choices should be songs that non-Christians will find inspirational and thought provoking but nonthreatening. Stay away from songs that will make non-Christians feel condemned or guilty. And stay away from songs with lots of Christian jargon. The songs should be upbeat and positive with lyrics that describe the joy of being a Christian.

Many times, especially in the intimate setting of a coffeehouse, it's appropriate for musicians to share about the music they're playing. Encourage the women to talk to the audience about why the music they're playing or singing is important to them. The women's ministry musicians should also be trained in how to share their faith with a non-Christian so they can share their faith with individuals during set breaks.

Make arrangements for the group to provide music at various local venues. Have the musicians display a sign that explains that they're sponsored by the women's ministry at your church. Make sure the women have brochures about the programs at your church, as well as evangelistic devotionals or literature that they can pass out to those who are interested.

IDEA 10
late-night study spot

This is a fantastic idea if there's a college or university in your community.

Offer a room in your church as a free, late-night study spot for college women. Advertise in the women's dorms or halls. You might have the facility available from eight to midnight one or more nights during the week.

Set up tables and chairs in a room and offer coffee, tea, and hot chocolate, along with snacks such as cookies or cheese and crackers.

At least two women from your church should host this event together. If you're concerned about safety, invite a man from your church to be present as well. By all means, take whatever precautions you need to in order to be safe during this event!

Place brochures listing all of the women's ministry programs at your church near the door. Make sure to include information about college ministry programs at your church.

Set up an area in one corner of the room for prayer. Have one of the women staffing this event hang out at the prayer corner. Place a sign near the front of the room explaining that this woman is available to pray with them or to discuss spiritual matters.

IDEA 11
community meetings

Arrange to have several of your church's women's small-group Bible studies in your church meet in public places such as restaurants, libraries, or community centers. Older women might have their meetings in the cafeterias of retirement homes or even assisted-living facilities.

Have the same group meet at the same place on an ongoing

basis. The staff at the restaurant or community center will get to know the women in the Bible study group. Encourage women to engage in conversation with the staff. Over the course of time, have the women extend invitations to the women who work in the facilities where they meet. The invitations should be to fun, nonthreatening fellowship events.

IDEA 12
neighborhood groups

Encourage each woman in your group to get to know her neighbors well. She can begin by handing out Christmas cookies during the holidays or stopping to chat with a neighbor during a walk in the summertime.

Each woman from your group should intentionally work on friendships with her women neighbors. Stay-at-home moms can form a neighborhood play group for the children. Working women can start a car pool and offer to run errands for other working women. Older women can suggest a weekly card game or coffee get-together. Almost any woman can suggest a neighborhood walking group.

As the women build sincere relationships with others, have them begin to invite these women to come to women's ministry events. Provide training on friendship evangelism to help women know how to share their faith naturally with others.

IDEA 13
free gift-wrapping

During the holidays, offer free gift-wrapping at the mall or at local discount stores. Be sure to make arrangements for the free gift-wrapping with the management of the business.

Provide the wrapping paper, tape, scissors, ribbons and bows, gift tags, and the labor. Post a sign to explain that you're from the women's ministry group at your church.

You may also want to provide free hot chocolate and cookies so that your customers are likely to stick around the booth while you're wrapping their presents.

Have lots of literature available for people to look over while they wait for their packages. Include brochures on all the ministries of your church. Also set out free devotional books and Bibles. (Several Bible publishers offer very reasonably priced Bibles by the case for use in outreach.) Be sure information is available about how to contact people from your church who are willing to talk to people about spiritual matters.

IDEA 14
free baby-sitting

Arrange to have free baby-sitting in your church's nursery and children's facilities one evening or one day of the week. Coordinate this activity with the nursery staff at your church. Recruit women from your women's ministry program to staff the nursery. Be sure to abide by your church's health and safety policies for child care.

Advertise the baby-sitting service around the church's neighborhood and in local stores. Encourage women to drop off their children for care while they run errands or just take a break. Be sure to get the parents' and children's names, addresses, home phone numbers, allergy information, and emergency contacts. Make sure the moms know when they need to pick up their children.

When women come to pick up their children, give each woman a packet of information about your church's ministries. Also give her a warm, personal, friendly invitation to a specific women's ministry event.

IDEA 15
howdy neighbor!

Print brochures that describe in detail all the ministries of your church, as well as who to talk to at your church about spiritual matters or counseling issues. You may also want to include a devotional or a Bible.

Send the women from your women's ministry in groups of three to the houses that surround your church. Groups of three are better than groups of two because, if a woman were to get injured, one woman could stay with her while another woman went for help.

Have the women knock on each door, introduce themselves by name and as members of your church, and hand out a packet of information about your church with a very warm invitation to attend your church's worship service or some other event.

Many churches leave information at homes, but few people take the time to ring the bell and introduce themselves. But in today's society, many people are hungry for relationships. Do have group members introduce themselves at each house. It will help women get over being scared to approach others and talk about spiritual things. And it will also help your church's neighbors know that the people who go to your church are normal, friendly, everyday people.

IDEA 16
helping hands

Make arrangements at a Christian day-care center or preschool to pay a certain amount toward every child's care. For example, perhaps you could pay five dollars for every child.

Draw a hand on a sheet of paper. Inside the hand, type these words, using your own church's name: "The women at First Church wanted to give you a helping hand!" Photocopy the sheets. Clip the sheets to brochures about your women's ministry programs, and ask the staff at the day-care center to give each family one of the packets.

IDEA 17
thrift store funds

Make arrangements at an area thrift store to provide five-dollar coupons to women shoppers on a specific day.

First decide how much money you'd like to spend. For example, your group may decide it wants to spend $250. At five dollars each, you'll be able to help fifty women and invite them to your church.

Print up coupons that say something like "This coupon gave you $5 off your purchase today, compliments of the women's ministry at First Church." Attach the coupons to brochures that describe all of your church's women's ministries.

Have the thrift store stack the coupons at the cash register. As women customers come through the line, have the store clerk take five dollars off the total price of their purchases and put a coupon and brochure into the women's bags.

IDEA 18
free dinners

Once a week, hold a free dinner at your church for the neighborhood. This is an especially great idea if you live in an inner-city area or an under-resourced area.

Serve inexpensive, nutritious meals. For example, serve barbecued-beef sandwiches with chips, carrot sticks, apples, and cookies. Other ideas include chili, spaghetti, sloppy Joes, chef salads, chicken and rice, and vegetable beef soup. During the summer, set up barbecue grills and grill burgers and hot dogs.

As much as possible, make the food from scratch, and encourage the women from your church to donate their time and funds to buy the food.

Advertise around the neighborhood by taking fliers door to door.

At every table, place information about all your ministries.

Plant women or families from your church around the room, and make sure they know that their job is to get to know the people from the neighborhood who don't already come to your church. Have the church people warmly invite neighborhood people to come to a service.

IDEA 19
community discussions

Rent a room at a community center or at your local library, and hold a discussion on spiritual topics that would be of interest to unchurched women in your town. For example:

- Why are Christians so weird?
- Is God against women?
- Is God male or female?
- Why aren't there more women ministers in the church?

Invite several women from your church to lead the discussions. Work as a group to form discussion questions and to investigate what the Bible says about each issue.

Advertise the event in your local newspaper. You can also pass out fliers around the community and put signs in local businesses.

During the discussion, have the women from your church promote a lively discussion by asking what each woman thinks about the issue. Be sure that the discussion facilitators are open, warm, and friendly to non-Christians. This is a time to encourage dialogue and open discussion. This isn't a time to pass judgment or to be dogmatic about Scripture. Remember that women who don't know the Bible and who haven't put their faith in Christ can't be expected to submit to Scripture's authority and truth. The purpose of these talks is to encourage open discussion and to make friends with unchurched women in order to love them into your church.

Be sure that the discussion facilitators invite the women who attend to come to the events at your church.

IDEA 20
festival booths

Every community or county has festivals and fairs throughout the year. Rent booth space, and set out information about your church's women's ministries. Provide something free. Here are some ideas.

• A beverage. Give away free bottled water or soda in the summer or free hot chocolate during the winter.

• Prayer. Provide slips of paper for people to write their prayer requests on. Have women from your church pray for those requests. Or have the women pray with those who would like someone to pray with them personally.

• Free food. Is there a cultural delicacy that your church is known for? Make a lot of it, and give it away.

• Free stuff. You can give away key chains, bandannas, or sunglasses. Attach the name, address, and phone number of your church to anything you give away.

IDEA 21
congregational outreach

Chances are there are many women in your own church who don't attend women's ministry events and activities. Make sure they feel welcome by inviting them.

Attach invitations to a women's ministry event to fresh flowers, one invitation per flower. Have several friendly members of your women's ministry team stand outside in the church lobby before and after one week's worship services. Give these women baskets full of the invitation flowers so they can hand a flower to each woman they see. Make sure they also extend a very warm verbal invitation to the event.

IDEA 22
single women welcome

Many single women don't feel welcome at women's ministry events. Classes and social events for singles are often planned by another group within the church, so single women may never get to know the married women in their church even when they're about the same age.

Make sure that your women's ministry program is welcoming to singles. Most importantly, plan events that don't cater only to married women or to women with children.

Have representatives from your women's ministry team visit several single's events and classes in your church. Have the representatives hand out sheets of paper and ask the single women to jot down things they'd like to see the women's ministry group do.

Also have the women's ministry representative talk about upcoming events and personally welcome the single women to come.

Consider getting single women involved in your planning teams or leadership team. They have a unique perspective on ministry in the church, and they have great gifts that would benefit your ministry.

IDEA 23
star parties

Creation theory isn't taught in the public schools anymore, and as a result, many children have lost a sense of wonder about the world around them. Hosting a star party once or twice a year will help the families in your community connect with nature and with the Creator.

Invite families in your community to your church parking lot, and have a Christian astronomer (professional or amateur) talk about the stars, the moon, and the wondrous creation of the night sky. You may want to have telescopes available so everyone can get a better look. The program need not last longer than a half hour.

Have the women's ministry serve refreshments after the presentation. Cookies in the shape of stars and half moons would be a hit! Give packages of glow-in-the-dark stars to all the children.

Send home brochures about God's creation of the world. Also send home information about your church's other ministries.

IDEA 24
short-term missions

There are lots of opportunities available for women to go on short-term mission trips.

For example, maybe your group could paint and wallpaper a home for pregnant teenagers. Perhaps your group could build a home in Mexico, or maybe your group could clear a vacant lot in an inner-city neighborhood or host a vacation Bible school at a Native American reservation.

Mission trips can easily be a part of your women's ministry programs every year.

Connect with the Christian agencies in your community and state to find out what needs they have that the women in your church could fill. For other ideas, contact your denominational headquarters or the individual missionaries that your church supports both at home and abroad.

IDEA 25
neighborhood prayers

Send women door-to-door all over your community to pray for and with the citizens of your town.

The women should go out in threes—it's safer than going in pairs.

Have the women take clipboards with them, along with brochures about your church.

Have the women knock at every house. They should stay outside the house on the front porch, introduce themselves by their first names, say what church they are with, and ask whoever has answered the door if he or she has any prayer requests that they can pray for. Have one person write down the requests, while one of the other women talks to the person at the door. Then the women should ask, "Would it be OK if we prayed for you right now?"

If the person says yes, one woman should quickly pray aloud for him or her right then. If the person says no, the women can indicate that they'll pray later in the day. The women should then give the person a church brochure and be on their way. If the person who answered the door didn't have any prayer requests, the women can still give him or her a brochure before moving on.

The women should go door-to-door for an hour or so. Then they should go to a park, to the church, or to one of their homes to pray for all the requests they received.

IDEA 26
sharing Christ with others

It can be very intimidating to share your faith with others. But it gets easier with practice. Use this series of easy meetings to train the women in your group to talk about Jesus with others.

✿ **Meeting 1:** Meet with a small group of five or six women who'd like to learn how to talk to others about Jesus. Ask the women to begin by writing the story of how they became a Christian. Then have them get with a partner from the group, read their stories, then find another partner to read their stories to until they've read their stories to every other woman in the room. Encourage the women to ask each other questions to help them clarify their stories.

Homework assignment: The women should each tell five people how they became a Christian. At this point, have the women simply tell their friends and family the story.

✿ **Meeting 2:** Talk first about the homework assignment. At this point, women should have practiced telling their stories at least ten times with people they feel comfortable with. Next, have each woman think of three things God has done in her life. Have women write a story about each of the three things. Then have the women pair up with one partner after another, just as they did last week, to tell each other their stories.

Homework assignment: Have the women tell five people one of their stories. Also have the women look for one thing God is doing in their lives each day this week and write it down in a way that can be shared with others. Have the women begin to collect all their stories in their own notebooks.

✿ **Meeting 3:** Talk about the homework assignment. Ask about their experiences telling friends and family about what God is doing in their lives? Ask if they were more aware of God's work in their day-to-day lives? Have each woman tell the entire group how God has worked in her life the past week.

This week, have the women come up with objections that others might make, thoughts that would hinder belief in Jesus. For example, some people say, "I could never believe in a God that allows so many people to suffer," or "I could never be a Christian—they're all hypocrites," or "But I don't understand why Jesus' death does anything for me." Have the women practice coming up with responses to all of the questions and objections they can think of. Have them do this through role-play rather than just talking about what they might say if they were ever to find themselves in that situation.

Homework assignment: By now, the women have gathered a collection of stories about how God is working in their lives. Have them find one non-Christian friend or acquaintance and tell that person one of their stories. Also have the women continue to work on stories about how God works in their lives and continue to put their stories in their notebooks.

✿ **Meeting 4:** Have the women first report about their homework encounters—what went well, what didn't go well, and how her friends or acquaintances reacted? Also have the women tell one another their new stories about how God has worked in their lives.

Next, have the women think of conversation starters that would help open a conversation about God. For example, maybe an acquaintance comments, "It seems like the world has gone completely crazy, what with all this terrorism!" or maybe a stranger says, "You're awfully cheery today. Are you always this happy?" Have the women spend the meeting time coming up with conversation starters and role-playing their responses.

Homework assignment: Bring God into conversations with at least three strangers or acquaintances. Continue collecting God stories for their notebooks.

Additional Meetings: Encourage the women to continue meeting to practice talking about Jesus and to encourage one another to keep talking about Jesus with others. Suggest that they make it a goal to tell someone about Jesus every day.

IDEA 27
international families

Many families travel to the United States because either the husband or the wife is pursuing university studies. It can be hard for the women in these families to make friends and become integrated into the community.

If there's a university in your community, find out what nationalities are represented there. Visit these women, and personally invite them to come to your church's women's ministry events and programs.

Also find out what needs these women have. Do they need furniture? training in English? help with locating good shopping places? Form a group within your women's ministry to connect these women with the resources they need. Take time to learn about their cultures. Make friends with them and love them. Then share Christ with them.

IDEA 28
visiting prisoners

Women in prison are often without friends and family. Work with the administrators of your local prison or jail to start a pen-pal ministry. Find women who enjoy writing letters, and connect them with women inside the prison who would enjoy receiving letters.

Encourage the women to write to the prisoners at least twice a month, if not once a week. As the women begin to develop relationships, have the church women gently begin to introduce the topic of God into the letters they write. All that they write about faith should be full of grace and love. Encourage the women to share their own faith in Christ and to lead the women prisoners toward putting their faith in Christ.

Find out what kinds of materials can be sent into the prison. If it's allowed, send Bibles and devotional materials to the women who seem interested.

Then begin visiting the women in jail. Visit frequently and pray with the women and help them answer their questions about God.

IDEA 29
gospel presentation

Don't assume that the women who regularly attend your events have put their trust and faith in Christ. Make regular presentations of what it means to be a Christian. Here are some ideas.

• Have an "altar call." Explain what it means to be a Christian, and then offer women the opportunity to give their lives to Christ. Ask them to come forward so that other women can pray with them.

• Have a drama team present a skit that shows a woman confessing her sins to God, asking for his forgiveness, expressing her belief in what Jesus has done for her, and asking God to take over her life. At the end of the skit, tell the women in the audience that if they've never done this before, they can do it today.

• Invite all the women to come forward to dedicate themselves to Christ. Put a large cross at the front of the room, and provide pens, pins, and slips of paper. Have all the women write a word that represents something they need to confess or something they'd like to express to God. Then ask the women to come forward and pin their words to the cross. Explain that for Christians, this is a time to affirm their decision to follow Christ. For non-Christians, this can be a time to put their faith in God for the first time.

• Give a PowerPoint presentation to show what Christianity *isn't* compared to what it *is*. For example, it's not about being perfect, but about being forgiven; it's not about memorizing all of the Bible, but about loving God's Word and following what it says. End the presentation with a clear explanation of how to confess, repent, and trust.

IDEA 30
retirement-home visits

Older people who are contemplating the end of life often find themselves thinking about spiritual matters that didn't interest them when they were younger.

Train a group of older women in your church to share their faith in Christ with others. Then encourage this group of women to visit nursing homes and retirement centers regularly and talk with the women there about faith matters. The women can approach the residents in these facilities by simply asking, "Do you have time for a little visit?"

After the women spend a few minutes chatting, the woman from your church should ask, "I'd like to pray for you. Would that be OK with you? Is there anything special that I can pray about for you?" The woman should pray for the resident and then ask one of these questions to turn the conversation to spiritual things:

• Have you put your faith in Jesus?

• Do you have any questions about what it means to be a Christian?

• Would you like to know how you can have eternal life in heaven?

• Do you have questions about God that worry or bother you?

Encourage these women to visit the retirement home or nursing home frequently so that they become friends with the residents. A woman may only open up to talking about spiritual matters after she feels she's talking to a true friend.

IDEA 31
light of the world

This is a great idea to use at Christmas.

You'll need a large collection of votive candles and votive candleholders.

Print fliers that say, "Find out more about the Light of the World. Visit [your church name goes here]." Add information about your church's Christmas programs and regular church ministries.

Gather a group of women to go Christmas caroling. Have each woman bring a large candle in a holder with a glass chimney. Bring along baskets with the extra votive candles, candleholders, and the fliers.

The women should go from house to house, each woman holding her own lit candle, and sing two sacred Christmas carols at each home. As the carolers approach each home, one person should put a votive candle in a candleholder and light the candle. During the last verse of the last song, give the lit votive candle, along with the flier, to the resident. Then say, "Merry Christmas!" and move on to the next house.

IDEA 32
springtime tussie mussies

This is a wonderfully elegant way to invite women to a springtime outreach event.

Use stiff paper and strong tape or a stapler to create small paper cones, otherwise known as tussie mussie holders. The patterned paper sold at scrapbook stores is perfect for these holders.

Punch two holes in either side of each tussie mussie holder, and tie a ribbon through the holes to act as a hanger.

Line each cone with a frilly paper doily. Then put a small bouquet of spring flowers in each cone to make a tussie mussie. Attach a note inviting women to a women's ministry spring event.

Hang the tussie mussies on the front doors of women you'd like to invite to a women's ministry event. ✿

section **eight**

retreats

Retreats are wonderful opportunities for women
to get away from their everyday responsibilities and to rest, have
fun, and spend some concentrated time learning about God. And
for many women, retreats provide the only time they really have
to themselves with no children to care for, no meals to plan, and
no chores or responsibilities pressing on them.

Retreats can require a lot of planning, but they're well worth
the effort. Retreats offer women a chance to take a long pause to
reflect on their lives and where they are in their relationships
with God. Retreats give women time to see others in a relaxed
and fun setting. Spending a whole weekend together without
the distractions of home, work, and family gives women the
time to make new friends and to deepen the friendships they
already have.

You'll find plenty of ideas in this section to help you develop
retreats that are powerful, life-changing events. These ideas will

make the planning easier and the spiritual lessons more meaningful. You'll also find lots of theme ideas to spark your creativity as you plan retreats for the women in your church.

IDEA 1
basic retreat planning

Planning a retreat is a big job with lots of details to manage. Here are some hints to make it a little easier.

Form a committee. Recruiting volunteers for the committee a year before the retreat will leave you plenty of time to plan. You'll need people to be in charge of location and accommodations, recreation and fellowship, food, budget, publicity, and teaching. You may also want to have women in charge of such things as decorations and small-group discussion material.

Planning the retreat has to begin by coordinating three core elements of your retreat.

1. Choose a theme for the retreat. You'll need to know what your theme is so that you can find speakers to teach within the framework of your theme.

2. Find a speaker. You'll need to determine whether you'll hire a speaker or use teachers from your church. If you choose to hire a speaker, you might check online sources for women who can speak about your theme. Just type "women's ministry speakers" into a search engine to find several sources of information. Your regional denominational office can probably suggest speakers, and women's ministry directors at other churches in your area might also have ideas. If you're holding your retreat at a Christian camp, chances are the camp's staff will have a listing of possible speakers.

3. Find a location. Choose a location that's affordable and within an easy traveling distance. Make sure that the accommodations are suitable for your group. Some women will feel more comfortable in a resort or hotel setting; others don't mind roughing it in bunk beds or dormitories. Check that the location can accommodate the number of women you expect at the retreat.

The date of your retreat will depend on the availability of your location, the availability of your speaker, and all the other events on your church's calendar.

Once you've got teachers and a location firmed up, you can start working on the funds. Determine how much you'll need to charge for the event based on speaker fees, room rates, and recreation costs. Here are some other questions you'll need to consider. Will the church be providing funds for any of these things? Will you need to plan fundraisers throughout the year? Will the women be paying all the costs themselves? Do you need to make arrangements to provide scholarships for some women?

Once you know the cost, the speakers, the theme, the date, and the location, you can begin to publicize the event. There are lots of ways to get the word out about your retreat. Be sure to put announcements in the bulletin and display posters in the hallways and in the women's bathrooms at your church. Announce the retreat from the pulpit during worship services, as well as at every women's ministry event. You may also want to print brochures/registration forms that can be mailed to each woman's home.

Planning exactly what will happen during the retreat will take a lot of thought as well. Having a basic idea of what you'd like to accomplish at the retreat, as well as what recreational opportunities are available at your location, will help you plan. Check out the suggested retreat schedule on page 202. Mark out the things you don't want to include, and add in the other things that you do want to include. In addition to your teaching times, you'll want to be sure to provide plenty of down time for rest and recreation. And you'll also want to provide some structured fellowship time to help women get to know one another. Another priority might be to include time for each woman to be alone with God.

Beyond these basics, you'll want to plan for some extra-special touches. You might decorate the meeting rooms to go along with the retreat's theme. If your budget allows, print workbooks for the retreat. Include schedules of the various teaching times and space for journaling. Another nice touch is to give away little gift bags that go along with the theme. For example, if your retreat has a gardening theme, you could put a sample size of Burt's Bees lotion and an inexpensive pair of gardening gloves in the bag. You can leave the gift bags in each woman's room or hand them out at the first meeting.

IDEA 2
suggested schedule for weekend retreats

Friday Night

6:00-7:00 p.m.	Dinner
7:00-7:30	Getting-to-Know-You Activities
7:30-8:00	Praise and Worship
8:00-8:30	Quick Devotion
8:30-9:00	Small Group Discussions
9:00-10:00	Snacks and Fellowship
10:00	Roommate Prayers and Lights Out

Saturday

7:30-8:30 a.m	Breakfast
8:30-9:00	Personal Devotions and Prayer time
9:00-9:15	Break
9:15-9:45	Praise and Worship
9:45-11:15	Teaching Time
11:15-12:00	Small Group Discussions and Prayer
Noon-1:00 p.m.	Lunch
1:00-5:00	Recreation
5:00-6:00	Dinner
6:00-6:30	Praise and Worship
6:30-8:00	Teaching Time
8:00-8:45	Small Group Discussions
8:45-9:00	Break
9:00-11:00	Movie and Snacks
11:00	Roommate Prayers and Lights Out

Sunday

7:30-8:30 a.m.	Breakfast
8:30-9:00	Personal Devotions and Prayer time
9:00-9:15	Break
9:15-9:45	Praise and Worship
9:45-10:30	Teaching Time
10:30-11:00	Small Group Discussion and Commitment Time
11:00-11:15	Praise and Worship, Concluding Remarks
11:15	Check Out (and head home)

IDEA 3
tabletop discussions

Retreat time is precious. Make use of mealtimes to help women get to know one another better and to apply what they're learning to their daily lives by providing tabletop discussion questions. At each meal, put a list of discussion questions on each table. Encourage women to sit with different women at every meal and to use the discussion questions to get to know one another better. Include a variety of questions—some silly, some thought provoking, some personal, and some about the theme.

IDEA 4
small retreats

Organizing a large retreat can be an organizational challenge for your retreat committee. Women can sometimes find it hard to really relax and experience God's presence when they're with a hundred or more women. As an alternative to the large retreat, consider hosting a series of smaller retreats for no more than fifteen to twenty women.

Having smaller retreats will allow women to experience greater quiet and rest. They'll be able to enjoy a more intimate setting and get to know a few women really well. Scheduling several smaller retreats will also give women more flexibility in choosing a convenient time to go.

You can use the same theme and teaching sessions at all of the retreats as each woman will only be attending one retreat. While you probably won't be able to hire a speaker for a series of retreats, you can use a Bible study series or a video curriculum. The learning that happens at these retreats will be more personal, more interactive, and more discussion-based. This kind of teaching will also help to increase the intimacy and relationship-building that happens. Smaller retreats also mean that you won't need a huge leadership team to attend each retreat. One or two leaders will be plenty.

IDEA 5
retreat centers

Consider holding your retreat at a retreat center at a monastery or abbey in your area. The retreat center has a ton of advantages. Many monasteries or abbeys have retreat coordinators who've already done the planning. They have spiritual exercises, recreation, and meals already planned and ready for your group to enjoy. These retreat centers often focus on prayer and other simple spiritual disciplines that will help the women in your church connect with God on a very deep and intimate level.

These retreat centers are often very affordable. While they aren't fancy or luxurious, they provide clean yet simple accommodations and plain, filling, nutritious food, allowing the women in your group to concentrate on God. Another advantage is that these centers provide another perspective on living the Christian life. Worshipping God in a tradition that's different from your own can be refreshing, and experiencing a bit of the simple life of cloistered Christians can provide new insights into being a devoted Christian in the hectic modern world in which we live.

IDEA 6
roommate discussion groups

Attending a retreat alone or with just one or two friends can be intimidating, especially if the retreat is large.

Have the women who share rooms become small discussion groups, and provide topics for them to discuss each night before bedtime. These discussions will allow the women to process and debrief the information that was presented during the day. The small groups also help women open up about how God is speaking to them. Spiritual discussions don't always happen naturally, but forming roommate discussion groups is a great way to prompt them among women who may be too shy to talk about spiritual things on their own.

A side benefit is that the small discussion groups will help women form deeper friendships with one another.

IDEA 7
video retreat

If you're on a small budget and you've got a small group, consider using a video curriculum, rather than hiring a speaker, to provide the teaching for your retreat. These curriculum products supply discussion guides to go along with the videos. Schedule sessions for watching the video, and plan plenty of time to go through the discussion guide so women can dig into the Word of God and discuss the topic with one another.

If your group is too large to gather around one television, provide several sessions. Form smaller groups of ten to fifteen women, and rotate them through the schedule. Groups that aren't watching the video can be enjoying recreational activities or craft activities. Or they can be enjoying a prayer time or a praise and worship time.

IDEA 8
follow-up learning

Retreats are often an intense time of learning and change—they're the mountaintop experiences. It can be tough to maintain that change, and even the enthusiasm of the retreat, after the retreat is over. Be very purposeful about the learning experiences you plan after a retreat. You may want to send each woman home with a devotional or a personal Bible study guide that she can work through at home to enhance what was covered at the retreat. You may want to have each woman's small Bible study group continue to talk about the experience and continue learning about the themes studied at the retreat. Another great idea is to plan service experiences to help the women put into practice what they've learned.

RETREAT THEMES

Here are some general theme ideas to help you plan your own retreats. (These themes are also useful as banquet themes!)

THEME 1
aloha from the heart

This tropical-themed retreat is perfect for the cold, dismal months of fall and winter. You can find large photomurals of tropical scenes at some department stores to use as a backdrop for the platform area for the speakers. Add atmosphere with lots of houseplants and potted palm trees. Decorate the tables with grass skirts, and have all the leaders bring in their patio umbrellas to add to the ambiance.

Encourage all the leaders to wear tropical shirts or dresses. Provide a lei for everyone who attends. Serve pineapple juice mixed with ginger ale, and put little umbrellas in the glasses. Have the speakers talk on building relationships and having genuine love for others.

THEME 2
come grow with us

Decorate with posters or murals of large sunflowers. For props, use wheelbarrows and gardening tools. Have butterfly, honeybee, and flower helium balloons float on ribbons around the perimeter of the room. Use checked tablecloths, and for centerpieces, make silk flower arrangements and put them in watering cans. Give out flower seed packets as favors. Separate small groups by choosing a different flower for each group and using the flowers to decorate name tags. Have the speakers talk about personal growth and improving one's prayer and worship life.

THEME 3
passport to adventure: journey from the desert to the promised land

Put a tent on the stage, and place potted palms around it. Put a "Road Closed" sign in the corner of the stage in front of a backdrop of tall pyramids. String name tags on lanyards, and laminate the name tags so that the women can use them as luggage tags in the future. Design the retreat's "Schedule of Events" to look like a passport, and give a schedule to each attendee. As the women go from activity to activity, make arrangements for someone to "stamp" their "passports." At the end of the retreat, you can give prizes for the most stamps. Set up the registration desk to look like a customs office. Give each woman a small compass and a small nylon backpack filled with all the materials she'll need for the retreat.

THEME 4
alterations: are you ready to be altered?

This theme focuses women's attention on allowing God to make changes in their lives. Set the stage with flowing lengths of fabric hung from the ceiling and wrapped around several dressmaker forms. Cut name tags in the shape of a dressmaker form, and glue different kinds of fabric to the name tags to designate the different small groups. Make one of the special activities a fashion show of the season's current fashions. All of the leaders can wear tape measures around their necks to set them apart. Have the speakers discuss topics such as confession, repentance, and living by the Spirit.

THEME 5
bon appétit: lessons from meals with Jesus

Have the speaker focus on what can be learned from these four meals recorded in Scripture: the marriage feast at Cana, breakfast on the shore, the feeding of the five thousand, and the Last Supper. Decorate the stage simply with a beautifully set dining-room table and then change the props for each meal. For the marriage feast at Cana, use a wedding dress on a mannequin and a wedding cake that can be used for refreshments after the teaching time. Hang fishnets, and make a small, fake campfire on the stage floor to represent the breakfast on the shore. For the feeding of the five thousand, set out baskets of bread and fish. Decorate for the Last Supper by setting out communion elements, and have the group celebrate communion at the end of the teaching time.

THEME 6
puzzles: completing God's picture, one piece at a time

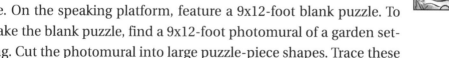

Have the speaker at this retreat focus on finding God's will for your life. On the speaking platform, feature a 9x12-foot blank puzzle. To make the blank puzzle, find a 9x12-foot photomural of a garden setting. Cut the photomural into large puzzle-piece shapes. Trace these puzzle-piece shapes onto a 9x12-foot section of butcher paper. Hang the butcher paper on a wall. As the retreat progresses, tape the puzzle pieces to the blank puzzle. The puzzle should be complete by the last session.

To make name tags, glue multiple puzzle pieces in a collage onto sturdy poster board. Use different colors of poster board for the backgrounds to designate different small groups. Have each small group work on a puzzle throughout the weekend.

THEME 7
new and improved: God's gift of renewal

This is a wonderful theme for a spring retreat. Have the speaker at this retreat focus on God's plan to renew us through Christ. She can use Scripture passages such as Revelation 21:5a and 2 Corinthians 5:17. To decorate, use bold colors and block letters to make signs that imitate the way cleaning products are advertised as being "New and Improved" or "Now With More Power!" For fun, have small teams of women develop advertising slogans to "promote" God's renewal and the way it changes them into the women he wants them to be.

THEME 8
20/20: catch the vision

This would be an excellent theme for a leadership planning retreat. Have the speaker talk about the importance of vision in ministry. Decorate the platform with a gigantic eye chart similar to one an optometrist would use. You may want to "hide" key words from the speaker's talk within the eye chart in the way that words are hidden in a word-search puzzle. Provide plenty of time for the women to pray and seek God's direction. Then plan plenty of time to discuss how your women's ministry should move forward in the coming years.

THEME 9
reflections: God's lessons recalled

This is a great theme to use during a fall retreat or an end-of-the-year retreat. Have the speaker talk about looking back at one's life to glean spiritual lessons from one's past. Decorate each table with mirror tiles and candles. Hang a large picture frame on the stage to act as a "mirror." Hang elements behind the frame that will relate to what the speaker talks about. For example, if the speaker talks about the lessons one learns from family, hang scrapbooks behind the frame. If the speaker talks about childhood, hang toys and children's clothes behind the frame. You can change the objects for each of the talks. Encourage the women to take the time to reflect on what's happened to them in the last week, the last year, or the last decade and to realize what God is teaching them through those events. This would be a great retreat for your church's scrapbookers to host a scrapbooking party!

THEME 10
waiting for God

This theme would work well for a retreat in the middle of winter when the earth rests and waits for spring. Have the speaker talk about patience, faithfulness, and the discipline of waiting for God to reveal his plan or to work in our lives or the lives of others. For decoration, put large bare tree branches in pots and put the pots around the platform area. Hang large pictures of clocks in different shapes and colors on the branches. Use pictures of different kinds of timepieces on the women's name tags to indicate which small groups each woman is in. It will be important during this retreat to plan time for the women to wait quietly on the Lord. Provide each woman with a notebook so she can write what God tells her.

THEME 11
joyful, joyful, we adore thee

Celebrate God's gift of joy with this fun-filled retreat. Decorate the platform with pictures of laughing and smiling people. Hang "joyful" words such as *joy, happy, cheer,* and *ha, ha, ha* from the ceiling. Have the speaker talk about what it means to lead a joy-filled life in Christ. Decorate tables with fun tablecloths in bright colors and patterns—no two need be alike. Sing upbeat songs. For the entertainment, consider hiring a Christian comedian. If you can't afford a comedian, rent funny movies. For the name tags, print jokes on the front of each woman's tag, but print the punch line on the back. The women can mingle, reading one another's name tags, but each woman will have the joy of delivering her punch line to every woman who reads her joke.

THEME 12
make me an instrument

For this retreat, the speaker should talk about how we are God's instruments in the world because God uses us to bring his peace, reconciliation, and love to the world. The speaker can use the references to the potter in Isaiah and Romans as the scriptural theme for the retreat. To decorate the platform, create several *tableaux vivants* of women using different kinds of instruments. For example, in one scene, have a woman pose playing a musical instrument. In another scene, women might pose as if using medical or scientific instruments, and in another scene, women might pose with a household "instrument" such as an iron. The women can pose for about five minutes before the speaker presents her teaching. You can collect various instruments or tools to use as centerpieces on the tables.

THEME 13
rest

This is a wonderful retreat theme any time of the year because all women need more satisfying times of rest. Have the speaker talk about the various meanings of rest in Scripture. Rest can be quite literal—God offers us rest away from the business of life. Rest can also be metaphorical—the New Testament speaks of salvation as a kind of rest. Place a large, comfy bed on the platform, and decorate the bed with lots of pillows, comfortable throws, and a frilly bed skirt. Use quilts or comforters as tablecloths. Provide time in the afternoon for naps, and plan to start things a little bit later than you normally would in the morning so that the women can sleep in a little and enjoy feeling rested as they start the day.

THEME 14
an (extra) ordinary life

Use the teaching times in this retreat to talk about how a simple and ordinary life presents us with countless opportunities for extraordinary faithfulness, devotion, and service to God. We may not all be called to be dynamic evangelists, prolific authors, or famous singers, but we are each called to live our lives with passionate devotion and radical obedience to our Lord. Decorate the platform with banners painted to look like an *Extra* sugarless gum package. Scatter *Extra* gum packages on the tabletops for a fun, casual table decoration. Attach different-colored gum wrappers to the women's name tags to designate the various small groups.

THEME 15
community of faith

At this retreat, emphasize the need to build community and relationship within the body of Christ. Provide lots of opportunities for women to interact and make friends. To decorate the platform area, tape life-size cardboard "gingerbread" people to the wall. You'll need one cardboard person shape per woman. Early in the retreat, provide time for the women to take a person shape and decorate it to look like themselves. Provide colored paper in solids and patterns, scissors, markers, and whatever else you think would help the women decorate the cardboard shapes. Tape the decorated shapes to the wall at the front of the room so that it looks as if they're holding hands. Talk about how, at the beginning of the retreat, the women didn't know one another and seemed colorless and without distinction. As the retreat continues, each woman's individuality shines through as the women get to know one another and become a community of friends who love and care for one another.

THEME 16
a grrreat life

Use a safari theme to decorate for this retreat. Make a large sign for the platform, using orange and black tiger stripes and the words "A GRRReat Life." Drape long panels of animal-print fabric from the ceiling, and place lots of potted plants on the platform too. Use similar animal-print fabric for tablecloths and to embellish name tags. If someone in your church has tribal masks or drums, you can use those too. Set the mood by playing CDs of African drum music. Have the teachers talk about what it means to have a rich, satisfying life in Christ. They might explain what the Bible means when it says that Christians are to live an abundant life. Teachers might also talk about contentment and about daring to live God's will through radical obedience. ❀

section **nine**

leader
HELPS

Being well organized and having a well-thought-out, well-prayed-through plan are the keys to having an effective women's ministry program that helps women grow in their love for Christ and others. This section is stuffed with great tips to help you do just that.

This section will help you work with your leadership team to think through the priorities for your women's ministry. You'll decide just what you'd like to accomplish and plan how to go about it. You'll also learn to bathe everything in prayer, seeking God's wisdom and direction in all your planning.

The section also includes tips for showing your leaders and volunteers just how much you appreciate them and the work they've done, as well as ideas to help your leaders grow spiritually.

You'll also find lots of helpful forms that you can photocopy for use in your church. There are forms to help you find volunteers and forms to help you evaluate your ministry events and programs.

Secrets of an Effective Women's Ministry

1. Pray and be sensitive to God's direction.

2. Evaluate the needs of the women in your church.

3. Develop a clear vision.

4. Communicate your vision first to your leaders and then to your entire group.

5. Establish credibility and trust with your leaders.

6. Develop clear standards for your team.

7. Believe in your leaders.

8. Love your people.

9. Develop a strong outreach program that anyone can participate in.

10. Provide training and opportunities to use and develop every woman's gifts.

IDEA 1
purpose wheel

Be very intentional about developing a purpose statement or mission statement for your women's ministry program. You'll use your purpose statement to evaluate every single program or event you're considering for the women in your church.

Your purpose statement should include a very clear goal. Ideally it will mention what you want women to experience or become and why that's important. For example, your purpose statement could be something like this: "We help women fulfill their biblical purpose by learning to love Jesus, making deep friendships with other Christians, and serving the world in Christ's name."

Once you've come up with your purpose, use it to help you plan activities and events. Here's how.

Write your purpose statement in the center of a piece of paper. Draw a small circle around the statement. Then draw a large circle around that small circle. Divide the large circle into as many facets as you have in your purpose statement. In the example above, you'd divide the circle into three sections: learning to love Jesus, making friendships, and serving the world. Decide what is the main purpose of every event you plan. Write each event in the appropriate section. See the example on the page 223 to see how a church might evaluate its programs.

Once you've sorted your events by purpose, you can evaluate whether your overall program is balanced. It'll be obvious at a glance if you planned too many fellowship activities or too many discipleship activities.

IDEA 2
before-the-event meal

When you've planned a big event for your women's ministry program, gather your leadership team, and go to a restaurant to enjoy a meal together before the event. If you've invited a special speaker for the event, take this time to fellowship with her. A special meal is a great way to help your team bond together. And it helps a speaker feel at home and welcome in your group. Enjoy a relaxing meal together, and just have fun chatting and laughing. End the meal with a time of prayer and dedicate the event to the Lord.

IDEA 3
first you pray

Form a prayer team. Have this team be in charge of finding volunteers to pray regularly for women's ministry events. Also have this team find volunteers to pray *during* every women's ministry event. Ideally, at least two women will pray during each event.

The prayer team can also take problems and questions to the Lord in prayer. When you're investigating whether to go in a new direction, have the prayer team petition God. Whether your decision is about what events to plan or what Bible study curriculum to use, ask God what he wants your church to do. Have your prayer team ask God for direction, for discernment, and for wisdom. Ask God to give you confirmation for the decisions you've made.

After the prayer team has brought your requests before God, patiently wait for God's answer. Encourage every pray-er to write down verses or thoughts that come to her after her prayer. Then have everyone share her sense of the Holy Spirit's direction. In time, you will all come to a common understanding of the direction your ministry should take. Only then should you go forward.

IDEA 4
leadership appreciation dinner

At the end of the ministry year, hold a special appreciation dinner or breakfast to honor those who've served as teachers and leaders throughout the year. An elegant dessert evening is another wonderful way to appreciate your leaders.

Make the evening's theme "Heroes of the Faith." Briefly speak about the heroes mentioned in Hebrews 11, and emphasize that the women who've faithfully served are heroes of the same caliber as those mentioned in Scripture.

Have each ministry coordinator write an appreciation card for the women who work under her. Have ministry coordinators call out each woman's name, one at a time, from the microphone so that women come to the front individually to receive the cards.

IDEA 5
leadership growth

Sometimes the leaders in a church's women's ministry neglect their own spiritual growth because they're so busy helping other women grow. Don't let that happen in your church! It's vitally important that all of us take time to meet with God and grow in our knowledge and love of him.

Gather your leaders together at least twice a year for a growth event you've planned just for them. At one of your get-togethers, you could introduce the theme for the year's women's ministry programs. Here's how that meeting might look if your theme was "Growing in the Knowledge of God."

Plan your meeting around a gardening theme. Decorate tables with red-checked tablecloths. Put terra-cotta pots of geraniums on the tables. Purchase sets of mini gardening tools as gifts for each leader. Find Bible verses about spiritual growth, and tie a verse to each of the tools. For dessert, serve dirt pots: mini terra-cotta pots filled with chocolate ice cream, crushed Oreo cookies, and gummy worms.

Use the teaching time to go through the parable of the sower and talk about the "soil" issues that are hindrances to personal spiritual growth. Give each leader a "gardening" journal so that she can use the journal to write about tending the garden of her soul. Encourage the women to make journaling a daily or weekly habit.

IDEA 6
publicity ideas

Good publicity is a really important part of a dynamic women's ministry program. Here are some ideas for "getting the word out."

✿ **Send a letter**—Send a welcoming letter to each woman in your church at the beginning of every women's ministry year. Explain the year's theme. Introduce the year's leaders. Tell the women about important dates they should mark on their calendar, such as holiday celebrations and the annual retreat. Issue a personal welcome to each woman. You can adjust this letter to be appropriate for women who don't attend your church and send it to women who visit your church.

✿ **Brochures**—Create lots of different kinds of women's ministry brochures. Have one brochure that highlights every women's ministry program and event. (You might want two versions of this brochure: one that's appropriate for women who attend your church and another version for outreach events.) Then have specialized brochures that highlight certain ministries in more detail. For example, you may want to have one brochure for Bible studies, one for special events, and one for service opportunities.

✿ **Newsletter**—If your church has a newsletter, be sure it includes lots of information about upcoming women's ministry events. But be aware that the contact list you've developed for women's ministry programs may be different from the general list the church office keeps. Consider cross-referencing the two lists to make sure that everyone on both lists gets a newsletter.

✿ **Posters and fliers**—Put posters and fliers describing women's ministry events in every classroom of your church. Also post them in hallways, in the fellowship hall, and at the entrances to the nursery and child-care centers.

✿ **Ministry booth**—Set up an information table where people gather before, between, or after worship services. Staff the table with friendly women who are truly knowledgeable about women's ministry programs. There's nothing more annoying than asking the information staff a basic question that they can't answer. The women at these booths should be trained to register women for upcoming events.

✿ **E-mail**—Send out women's ministry event information through e-mail. For example, you might send weekly announcements of what's going on in the women's ministry program. Personalize these by highlighting various people in the program.

✿ **Bathroom baskets**—Put baskets of brochures about your women's ministry programs on the counters in each women's bathroom in the church. Consider taping some of the brochures to the doors in the bathroom stalls.

✿ **Pulpit announcements**—Work with your pastor to provide time to showcase women's ministry announcements during the announcement time of the weekly worship service. Be sure to highlight each week's events in the worship bulletin, too.

✿ **Information for new people**—People who are new to your church won't understand your church's traditional events, clever event names, or abbreviations. Be sure to describe all your events so that someone who's never attended your church will know what's going on.

IDEA 7
needs survey

Use the survey on page 224 to help you plan programs for your ministry. Photocopy the survey, and pass it out at the beginning of the year. Make sure that new women are also given an opportunity to fill out the survey. Gather the surveys, tabulate the results, and use it to figure out which topics to offer as classes or Bible study sessions for your group.

IDEA 8
"i can help" survey

Use the survey on page 225 to learn about the talents and interests of the women in your church. Hand out this survey at the beginning of each women's ministry year. Also hand out this survey to new women in your group.

IDEA 9
applicant notice

When women apply for positions within your women's ministry, fill out the form on page 226, and send it to the other people on your church staff. Ask staff members to let you know if they have any concerns about any of the applicants. Taking care of some issues will simply be a matter of the staff member initiating a conversation with an applicant, and there will be no reason for you to be involved. But there are some issues that you will need to be made aware of.

IDEA 10
the big event countdown form

Make the countdown to a big event easy with the convenient planning checklist on page 227. Not only will you stay on task, but you can keep your co-workers informed of changes and progress.

Volunteers will appreciate the overview, and you'll have delegated yourself into smooth sailing!

Fill in the pertinent facts, and give a photocopy of this form to your committee chairpersons. Use this form to keep track of your progress, then file it to use as a basis for future planning.

IDEA 11
touching base

It can be hard to keep up with new faces in your group. Make a copy of the chart on page 228, and keep it in your day planner. List names of people you'd like to contact and why. Then, when you have a few spare moments, you'll be ready to give someone a quick call or send a quick e-mail.

You might also use this form for your leaders or your volunteers so you can touch base with them and see how things are going with the ministries they're involved with. Be sure to pray for each woman as soon as you've finished talking to her.

IDEA 12
expense reports

Every leader needs a simple way to keep track of expenses. Use the simple form on page 229. Photocopy it, attach the photocopies to small envelopes, and give the envelopes to all your volunteers. Have the volunteers write the expense on the form and put the receipt in the envelope. Make sure that everyone knows what kinds of expenses are reimbursable and how often expenses should be submitted.

IDEA 13
feedback form

Photocopy the form on page 230, and ask participants to use it to give you feedback about an event. You probably won't want to use this form for every event. But it's a great way to find out whether people have enjoyed a new event. You can gather all of the forms from an event and file them so that you can refer to them the next time you want to plan a similar event.

Consider each person's feedback very carefully. It's easy to get defensive or to write off someone's negative comments. Ask God to make you receptive to what the women tell you and to adjust your events and plans to meet people's needs.

IDEA 14
copyright permission form

There will be times when you'd like to photocopy material to use in your ministry. To make legal photocopies, you need to obtain permission from the publisher. Use the form on page 231.

Be sure the information you include is accurate. And be sure to give yourself plenty of time to receive a return response. (Four to six weeks is generally enough.)

Sometimes there is a charge for using the material: Pay the requested amount promptly.

IDEA 15
press releases

Sending a press release to your local newspaper is a great way to publicize your event. See the sample on the following page. Keep these things in mind when submitting a press release.

Newspapers often need to receive material several days or weeks in advance. Find out when your newspaper's deadline is, and send in your press release early.

Don't be wordy, and don't use churchy language. Include only the pertinent information about your event. The editor will cut any fluff you add, and will probably rewrite whatever you submit.

Be sure to include your name, address, phone number, and e-mail address so the editor can contact you to clarify the details or get more information.

IDEA 16
volunteer application

Use the form on page 232 for women who would like to volunteer in your women's ministry program. Keep plenty of forms on file, and hand them out to any women who might be interested in helping out. When you're ready to fill a post, be sure to interview each woman applicant to make sure that their skills match up with the role they're applying for. Talk to each woman about her relationship with Christ. Also contact all of the references.

IDEA 17
volunteer agreement and ministry descriptions

 Use the form on page 233 to help all of your volunteers understand their roles and their terms of service. You may also want to use the ministry descriptions on pages 234-238.

Fill out two forms for every volunteer. Take time to meet with each volunteer to talk about her particular role in the women's ministry at your church. Encourage all volunteers to sign both copies of the agreement. File one copy, and have each volunteer take one copy home.

At the end of the term of service, you can meet with each volunteer again and either sign her up for a second term of service or allow her to gracefully exit her post. ❁

Sample Press Release

FOR IMMEDIATE RELEASE

Date:_____

Church:_____

Contact person:_____

Phone number/e-mail address:_____

Event:_____

Date of event:_____

First Church will host a Christmas banquet for all women on Saturday, December 20, at 6 p.m., in the church's fellowship hall. The banquet will feature special music by the church's women's string quartet, as well as a drama program presented by the church's youth group.

The event costs $5 and is open to the public.

First Church is located at 5213 North Wyndham Road, Chelsea Springs. For more information, call 555-4265.

Purpose Wheel

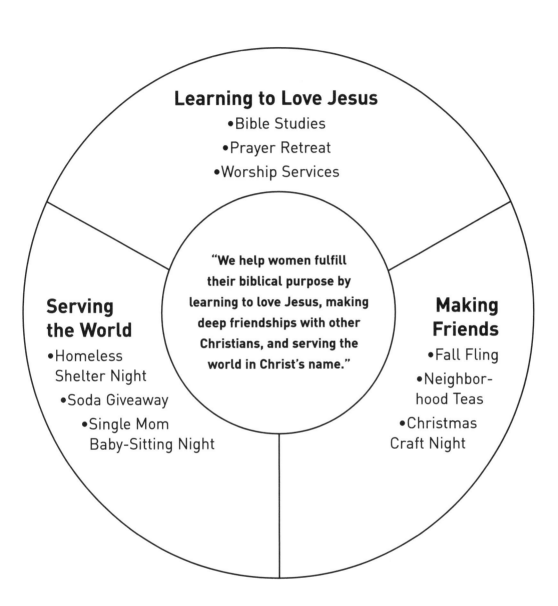

Learning to Love Jesus
- Bible Studies
- Prayer Retreat
- Worship Services

"We help women fulfill their biblical purpose by learning to love Jesus, making deep friendships with other Christians, and serving the world in Christ's name."

Serving the World
- Homeless Shelter Night
- Soda Giveaway
- Single Mom Baby-Sitting Night

Making Friends
- Fall Fling
- Neighbor-hood Teas
- Christmas Craft Night

Needs Survey

I would like to learn about (check all that apply):

- ❑ Eternal life
- ❑ Heaven
- ❑ The Holy Spirit
- ❑ God's attributes
- ❑ The Trinity
- ❑ The fruit of the Spirit
- ❑ Bible history
- ❑ Church history
- ❑ What this church believes in
- ❑ Biblical womanhood
- ❑ Joy
- ❑ Worry
- ❑ Contentment
- ❑ Trials and hard times
- ❑ Pride
- ❑ Loving God and others
- ❑ Spiritual disciplines
- ❑ Fasting

- ❑ What it means to be a church member
- ❑ How to avoid sin
- ❑ What to do about guilt
- ❑ Spiritual gifts
- ❑ How to have a relationship with Jesus
- ❑ How to pray
- ❑ How to study my Bible
- ❑ How to teach my children about God
- ❑ How to take care of myself (nutrition, fitness, skin care)
- ❑ How to build spiritual traditions in my home
- ❑ Other:_____
- ❑ Other: _____
- ❑ Other: _____

Here are some questions I have about God or about being a Christian:

1. _____
2. _____
3. _____
4. _____

I'd like to study these books of the Bible:

1. _____
2. _____
3. _____
4._____

Here are some needs I have that aren't being addressed in the women's ministry programs:_____

_____

_____

Here are some suggestions for changes and improvements in the women's ministry program:_____

_____

_____

_____

"I Can Help" Survey
Many hands make light work.

Here are some ways you can help the women's ministry at our church. Please check all the ways you'd be willing to pitch in and lend us your helping hand.

Don't worry! Checking a box doesn't mean you're committed! We just need to know what kind of resources we have right here in our own group to help us better plan our activities. We'll contact you about each service opportunity, and you'll have a chance then to sign up or gracefully decline.

❏ Lead a Bible study
❏ Be a mentor
❏ Be a "mentee"
❏ Write or design publicity pieces
❏ Do general office work
❏ Serve meals
❏ Plan and prepare meals
❏ Bring treats
❏ Speak at an event
❏ Facilitate a small-group discussion
❏ Decorate
❏ Be a hostess
❏ Be on a planning committee
❏ Shop for supplies
❏ Organize supplies

❏ Organize volunteers
❏ Provide transportation
❏ Contact new women on the phone
❏ Visit new women in their homes
❏ Be on a welcoming team
❏ Sing or play special music
❏ Lead group singing
❏ Work at a registration table
❏ Provide centerpieces
❏ Take photos
❏ Host an event in your home
❏ Lead a woman to Christ
❏ Provide child care
❏ Other: _____
❏ Other: _____

Name: _____

Address:_____

_____

Phone number: _____

E-mail address: _____

Notice of Women's Ministry
Volunteer Applicants

Date:_____

Memo to:_____

From:_____ Phone number: _____

Please review the list of names below. These women have applied to be volunteers within women's ministry program. If you have concerns about any of these women, please contact them and discuss your concerns by this date _____. If you feel it's necessary, please contact me to discuss the issues. And please honor these people's privacy and dignity by keeping these matters confidential.

Names:_____

_____

_____

_____

_____

_____

_____

_____

The Big Event

Title:_____

Date:_____

Time:_____

Purpose:_____
_____

Overall Budget:_____

The Plan:_____
_____
_____

Six Months Before:_____
_____

Three Months Before:_____
_____

One Month Before:_____
_____

Final Week:_____
_____

Day Before:_____
_____

The Big Day:_____
_____

The Event:_____
_____

Activities chair:_____   Publicity chair:_____

Phone number:_____   Phone number:_____

Budget:_____   Budget:_____

Food chair:_____   Decorations chair:_____

Phone number:_____   Phone number:_____

Budget:_____   Budget:_____

After the event:_____

Cleanup planned:_____

Worker appreciation:_____

Notes and workers for next year:_____
_____

Touching Base

Name	Phone Number/ E-mail Address	Date Contacted	Comments	Prayer

Expenses

Name:_____Organization or group:_____

Item	Cost	Project

Total expenses:_____Today's date:_____

Signature:_____

Expenses

Name:_____Organization or group:_____

Item	Cost	Project

Total expenses:_____Today's date:_____

Signature:_____

Feedback Form

	Yes	No
1. Did you like this event?	❑	❑
2. Would you enjoy doing this again?	❑	❑
3. Did you meet someone new?	❑	❑
4. Was the cost reasonable?	❑	❑
5. Would you invite a friend next time?	❑	❑
6. Did you learn something new about yourself?	❑	❑
7. Did you learn something new about God?	❑	❑
8. Did you get to know others in the group better?	❑	❑
9. Are you glad you came?	❑	❑

10. On a scale of one to ten, how would you rate this event?_____

11. If you had to describe this event in one word, what would it be?_____
_____

12. What did you like best about this event?_____
_____
_____
_____
_____

13. What did you learn during this event?_____
_____
_____
_____

14. What would you change about the event?_____
_____
_____
_____

15. What did you not like about this event?_____
_____
_____
_____

Copyright Permission Form

Name:_____

Address:_____

Phone number:_____

E-mail address:_____

Phone number:_____

Date:_____

Copyright owner:_____

Address:_____

E-mail address:_____

Attn.: Rights and Permission

Dear _____,

My name is _____, and I am a part of the women's

ministry at _____. Recently I enjoyed hearing/

reading_____. I would like to
_____[title of work]

request permission to use the material on page _____ for our

_____ . We plan to make _____ copies. We
_____[event]

will not charge for the copies we make.

    Thank you for your attention in this matter. Please contact me if you have questions or need additional information. I will anticipate hearing from you in regard to permission status, credit line, and any expected fee.

Sincerely,

_____

Volunteer Application

Name: _____ Phone number: _____

Address: _____

E-mail address: _____

Age: _____ I've been a Christian for…_____

My experience in women's ministry:

Special skills I'd like to share:

I'd like to be involved with these ministries and these groups of women:

I'm available

Monday: _____ Times: _____

Tuesday: _____ Times: _____

Wednesday: _____ Times: _____

Thursday: _____ Times: _____

Friday: _____ Times: _____

Saturday: _____ Times: _____

Sunday: _____ Times: _____

References:

Name: _____ Phone number: _____

Name: _____ Phone number: _____

Name: _____ Phone number: _____

Volunteer Agreement

Thank you for volunteering to help in our congregation's ministry to women. We value your willing spirit, your time, and your dedication!

As a volunteer in women's ministry, you have decided to be…

Visible in your service to the Lord.

Observant, looking for ways to be of help to others.

Loving to the women you serve.

Useful in your vision for women's ministry.

Necessary and dependable.

Trained and willing to learn more about Christian education.

Excited in your service to God.

Energetic in your outreach.

Responsible to God for guidance.

In return, the women's ministry leaders in the congregation agree to …

Pray for you.

Listen to your needs.

Advise you of meetings, training sessions, concerns, and joys.

Nurture you in your service.

My title is _____

My term of commitment is _____

My duties will include _____

For questions and concerns, I can contact:

Name: _____ Title: _____ Phone number: _____

Name: _____ Title: _____ Phone number: _____

Signature of Women's Ministry Director _____

Date _____ Phone number _____

Signature of volunteer _____

Date _____ Phone number _____

Women's Ministry Leaders, Coordinators, and Teams
Ministry Description

Position
Director

Purpose
Serve as leader of the women's ministry leadership team.

Primary Responsibilities
Provide overall vision for the church's women's ministry; recruit other women to join the women's ministry leadership team; give direction and guidance to other women's ministry leaders; schedule, plan, and lead meetings of leadership team; empower and unleash women's ministry leaders to creatively lead and minister in their areas of responsibility.

Reports to...
Senior Pastor or Adult Ministry Director

Time required each month
Depends on the size of church and women's ministry, if the ministry is just beginning or if it's already established, and the number of events the ministry holds annually. The time required could range from one to more than ten hours per week.

Term
If the women's ministry is just starting, the director should commit to a term of two to three years and consider renewing that commitment for a year or two after the initial start-up period. If the ministry to women is already established, the commitment can be two years—one year as an apprentice to the preceding director, and one year as the director.

Training
Work as an apprentice to the previous director; attend fellowship or denominational leadership conferences, as well as regional and national women's ministry conferences.

Qualifications, Skills, and Gifts
Commitment to allowing God to work in her life; desire to use qualities and gifts wherever God desires; senses a call to lead ministry to women; gets energized by leading others; possessing gifts of leadership, administration, and encouragement.

Benefits
Gain a better understanding of the issues women face and find personal satisfaction while serving in this leadership capacity; work with and form deep relationships with other Christlike and committed women in the church.

Women's Ministry Leaders, Coordinators, and Teams
Ministry Description

Position
Events Coordinator/Team Leader

Purpose
As women search for places to test the waters of women's ministry, this leader will provide various entry points where both newcomers and seasoned attendees feel comfortable, connected, inspired, and transformed.

Primary Responsibilities
Coordinate the planning and carrying out of programs, special events, projects, and other activities; integrate a variety of events (fellowships, small groups, retreats) into connected and meaningful programs; ensure that events line up with both women's ministry vision and overall church vision; create new events (outreach events, guest speakers, adventure activities, mother-son/daughter events, sports outings); work with Communication Coordinator to publicize upcoming events of the women's ministry; plan, organize, lead, and evaluate each activity or delegate these tasks to a team of equipped leaders as the ministry grows.

Reports to...
Women's Ministry Director

Time required each month
Depends on size of church and women's ministry, if the ministry is just beginning or if it's already established, and the number of events the ministry holds annually. Could range from one to more than ten hours per week. As the ministry grows, the Events Coordinator position will become a Team Leader position, overseeing coordinators/leaders of different women's ministry events.

Term
If the women's ministry is just starting, Events Coordinator/Team Leader should commit to a term of two to three years. If the ministry to women is already established, the commitment can be two years—one year as an apprentice to the preceding Events Coordinator, and one year as the Events Coordinator.

Training
Work as an apprentice to the previous Events Coordinator; identify needed training and communicate to Women's Ministry Director; attend appropriate fellowship or denominational leadership conferences, as well as regional and national women's ministry conferences.

Qualifications, Skills, and Gifts
Commitment to allowing God to work in her life; desire to use qualities and gifts wherever God desires; senses a call to plan events that will draw in women and minister effectively to them; possessing gifts of administration, leadership, encouragement, humility, and evangelism.

Benefits
Gain a better understanding of the issues women face and find personal satisfaction while serving in this leadership capacity; work with and form deep relationships with the leadership team and with other Christlike and committed women in the church.

Women's Ministry Leaders, Coordinators, and Teams
Ministry Description

Position
Communication Coordinator/Team Leader

Purpose
To promote the events and ministries of the women's ministry through personal contact, newsletters, e-mails, Web site, brochures, bulletin boards, signs, displays, artwork, and photos.

Primary Responsibilities
Advise and assist other women's ministry leaders with their communication and promotional needs within the congregation; coordinate the scheduling, writing, and creating of all forms of communication; distribute communication pieces; maintain ministry database; oversee ministry publicity tools.

Reports to...
Women's Ministry Director

Time required each month
Depends on size of church and women's ministry, if the ministry is just beginning or if it's already established, and the number of events the ministry holds annually. Could range from one to more than ten hours per week. As the ministry grows, the Communication Coordinator position will become a Team Leader position, overseeing coordinators/leaders responsible for communications and promotion of different events and activities.

Term
If the women's ministry is just starting, Communication Coordinator/Team Leader should commit to a term of two to three years. If the ministry to women is already established, the commitment can be two years—one year as an apprentice to the preceding Communication Coordinator, and one year as the Communication Coordinator.

Training
Work as an apprentice to the previous Communication Coordinator; identify needed training and communicate to Women's Ministry Director; attend appropriate fellowship or denominational leadership conferences, workshops, and seminars on publicity, marketing, promotions, and public relations; attend regional and national women's ministry conferences.

Qualifications, Skills, and Gifts
Ability to communicate and work well with others; a willingness to lead and assist in all areas of communication and promotion for women's ministry events and activities; ability to listen; experience with reporting; possessing gifts of administration and encouragement.

Benefits
See results of service as increasing numbers of women get involved in women's ministry events and activities; find personal satisfaction while serving in this leadership capacity; work with and form deep relationships with the leadership team and with other Christlike and committed women in the church.

Women's Ministry Leaders, Coordinators, and Teams
Ministry Description

Position
Connecting Coordinator/Team Leader

Purpose
As new women become active in women's ministry, it's important that they feel welcome and integrated into various activities and relationship building events. The Connecting Coordinator works to ensure that these needs of individual women are met.

Primary Responsibilities
Strengthen the bonds among women in the church by connecting them to appropriate spiritual and social groups within the women's ministry and in the overall ministry of the church; gather and maintain accurate information about group members; assess current spiritual, relational, and emotional needs of women.

Reports to...
Women's Ministry Director

Time required each month
Depends on size of church and women's ministry, if the ministry is just beginning or if it's already established, and the number of events the ministry holds annually. Could range from one to more than ten hours per week. As the ministry grows, the Connecting Coordinator position will become a Team Leader position, overseeing coordinators/leaders responsible for connecting manageable numbers of women into appropriate groups, ministries, and places of service.

Term
If the women's ministry is just starting, Connecting Coordinator/Team Leader should commit to a term of two to three years. If the ministry to Women is already established, this can be a commitment of two years—one year as an apprentice to the preceding Connecting Coordinator, and one year as the Connecting Coordinator.

Training
Work as an apprentice to the previous Connecting Coordinator; identify needed training and communicate to Women's Ministry Director; attend appropriate fellowship or denominational leadership conferences, workshops and seminars on assimilation, as well as regional and national women's ministry conferences.

Qualifications, Skills, and Gifts
A people person with good organizational skills and the ability to work with others; well-developed interpersonal and social skills; management skills of planning, directing, and communication; willingness to develop relationships with other women beyond the surface level, yet work largely behind the scenes rather than up front; ability to delegate and enable others; possessing the gifts of administration, helps/serving, wisdom/discernment, counseling.

Benefits
See results as increasing numbers of women find relevance in the church and in their own lives by plugging in to appropriate groups and places of service that meet their emotional, relational, and spiritual needs; find personal satisfaction while serving in this leadership capacity; work with the leadership team and with other Christlike and committed women and form deep relationships with them.

Women's Ministry Leaders, Coordinators, and Teams
Ministry Description

Position
Outreach/Service Project Coordinator/Team Leader

Purpose
To help the women's ministry reach out and share God's love with others through outreach activities, service projects, and mission opportunities; to work toward the goal of seeing more people come to make a faith commitment to Christ as Savior.

Primary Responsibilities
Gather and maintain information on opportunities to serve others—within the women's ministry, within the church, in the local community, nationally, and globally; coordinate and connect women to help meet these various needs.

Reports to...
Women's Ministry Director

Time required each month
Depends on size of church and women's ministry, if the ministry is just beginning or if it's already established, and the number of outreach events and projects the ministry desires to hold annually. Could range from one to more than ten hours per week. As the ministry grows, the Outreach/Service Project Coordinator position will become a Team Leader position, overseeing coordinators/leaders responsible for various outreach events or activities and service projects.

Term
If the women's ministry is just starting, Outreach/Service Project Coordinator/Team Leader should commit to a term of two to three years. If the ministry to Women is already established, this can be a commitment of two years—one year as an apprentice to the preceding Outreach/Service Project Coordinator, and one year as the Outreach/Service Project Coordinator.

Training
Work as an apprentice to the previous Outreach/Service Project Coordinator; identify needed training and communicate to Women's Ministry Director; attend appropriate fellowship or denominational leadership conferences, workshops, and seminars on local outreach and missions; attend regional and national women's ministry conferences.

Qualifications, Skills, and Gifts
Organized; good listening skills; ability to delegate, desire to see others make a faith commitment to Christ; possessing gifts of service, helps, administration, and giving.

Benefits
See results as increasing numbers of women seek ways to be involved in outreach and service projects; work with and form deep relationships with the leadership team and with other Christlike and committed women in the church; experience personal satisfaction and inspiration as women work to bring others to Christ and as others make personal commitments to Christ.

EVALUATION FOR
Women's Ministry in the 21st Century

ease help Group Publishing, Inc., continue to provide innovative and useful resources for min-
ry. Please take a moment to fill out this evaluation and mail or fax it to us. Thanks!

Group Publishing, Inc.
Attention: Product Development
P.O. Box 481
Loveland, CO 80539
Fax: (970) 292-4370

As a whole, this book has been (circle one)

not very helpful   *very helpful*

1   2   3   4   5   6   7   8   9   10

The best things about this book:

Ways this book could be improved:

Things I will change because of this book:

Other books I'd like to see Group publish in the future:

Would you be interested in field-testing future Group products and giving us your feedback?
f so, please fill in the information below:

me _____

urch Name _____

nomination _____ Church Size _____

urch Address _____

y _____ State _____ ZIP _____

urch Phone _____

nail _____